100 FAMILY ADVENTURES

F

FRANCES LINCOLN LIMITED

CONTENTS

INTRODUCTION

The idea for *100 Family Adventures* grew from wanting to spend more quality family time outdoors – walking, cycling, kayaking... simply doing things together as a family.

We were worried about our time-pressured lifestyle that persistently put a squeeze on our family time. We didn't want our children to grow up molly-coddled and wrapped up in cotton wool, preferring to spend their time indoors in front of a TV or computer screen rather than enjoying the great outdoors. We wanted them, instead, to be connected to nature as well as technology and to balance their screen time with plenty of green time. It is our hope that they grow up as bold individuals who grasp opportunities and who look for adventure and fulfillment in life.

So what is adventure? Well, it can be whatever you want it to be; but to us, adventure is all about pushing your comfort zones, trying new activities, or doing familiar activities in different ways. But remember, adventure is personal and there are no rights or wrongs – you can come up with your own definition.

The 100 adventures in this book are designed to encourage other families to get out and do things together, to help adults and children alike to push their own comfort zones – even if it is just a little. They are sorted into categories, for ease of reference, but are not presented in any particular order, so you can tackle them however suits you best.

Everyone loves a list, so we have organized the adventures as a checklist on the contents page so that you can find them in the book and also tick them off as you complete them, allowing you to keep a record of how many you do.

As a family, and as individuals, we feel happier being outdoors and spending time together. And what better way to get to know your children, and yourself, than by sharing the thrill and excitement of a family adventure?

Now it's over to you. Adventure is out there – you just have to go and find it!

TIM, KERRY, AMY AND ELLA

The Meek Family

TIM, KERRY, AMY
AND ELLA MEEK
(AND SALLY!)

WOODLAND

Learn some bushcraft skills such as building a shelter, cooking in the open air or making something from nothing. How about walking high among the treetops, sleeping in a log cabin or undertaking a night walk, in the company of nocturnal creatures like owls and rabbits?

BUSHCRAFT SURVIVAL SKILLS
SHELTER BUILDING

Learn some bushcraft skills and become at one with nature.

Shelter is one of the five basic human needs for survival and wellbeing. It provides us with protection from the elements and helps us with temperature regulation. While it is unlikely that you and your children are going to be building a shelter on which your survival depends, at least not in the short term, this project is a valuable exercise. For children, the experience of creating their own shelter allows them to appreciate that their counterparts around the world are not all necessarily fortunate enough to have these basic needs met.

That said, you can be confident that all involved in the exercise of building a home-made shelter will find it an enjoyable and rewarding experience.

Here are some different types of shelter to build:

SIMPLE TARPAULIN TENT

By using a piece of tarpaulin with guy ropes, two walking poles and a handful of pegs, you can make an effective tent. The size of the tarpaulin determines how many people you can 'home'. This tent (right) was made from a kids' shelter-building set and can be adapted to make a wide range of different shapes and sizes.

TARPAULIN AND HAMMOCK

This is a slightly more technical shelter to build, as it requires more equipment (a rope, tarpaulin and guys, pegs and a hammock), but is really not difficult to set up. String a rope between two trees (to act as a ridge pole), drape the tarpaulin over it and peg it down using long guy ropes; this is the canopy or 'roof'. Then suspend the hammock under the canopy, making sure it is flat and taut.

TIPS AND CONSIDERATIONS

- When building shelters in the wild, try not to chop down or break any living vegetation; encourage children to respect the living world.
- Children of all ages love to make dens and hideouts. Encourage this by giving them space and time in the outdoors, and help them get started by choosing a good location and suggesting a source of building materials.
- Den building kits such as Kidcampz are useful aids for creative den building and are ideal for indoor and outdoor environments.

DID YOU KNOW?

The oldest tree in the world is the Great Basin Bristlecone Pine from California.

AMY SAYS...

SIMPLE DEN When we make a den outside, we take two Y-shaped sticks and place them about 2m/2yds apart on a gentle slope, then join them together with another stick. Next, we stack twigs onto the gently sloped sticks and when we've worked up a sturdy base, we pile some bracken on top. Here (left) is a den we made together when we were younger

LEAF SPOTTING In the woods gather up some different types of leaves that are lying on the ground. Next search for various trees (with their leaves on) and try to identify the trees that the leaves came from.

ELLA'S JOKE

Why was the ladybird kicked out of the forest?

—

Because she was a litterbug!

BUSHCRAFT SURVIVAL SKILLS
COOKING

Another basic need that we humans have is food; we need to eat regularly and healthily in order to stay fit and well. There are several bushcraft skills associated with cooking on a fire that you can introduce to children, but the first thing you have to do is create a flame.

WAYS TO CREATE A FLAME

MATCHES Waterproof and windproof matches provide a quick, reliable solution.

LIGHTER FLINTS These 'fire starters' are cheap, reliable and compact. A knife blade can be used to create friction on the sparking stick. Children can use them safely.

DRILL AND BOW A classic tool used to create a flame by friction. It is quite technical to make and use, so therefore not ideal for children.

DID YOU KNOW?

Clovers are actually edible and can be eaten to help you survive in the wild!

CREATING A FIRE

The sparks you create need to fall on and ignite into some dry kindling material such as dried grass, cotton wool or birch bark shavings. Ideally the kindling should be placed on a platform of thin wood. Once you have a flame, start laying down small twigs in a criss-cross formation over the flames so that oxygen will be able to flow through the gaps in the twigs. As the twigs catch fire and the smoke increases, keep piling twigs onto the flames until you are happy with your fire.

SAFETY

Children must always be supervised and behave sensibly near fires. They should also avoid getting too close to the flames, especially if wearing fleecy clothing that is highly flammable. Make sure the supervising adult knows how to safely start, manage and put out fires, and that someone is first-aid trained. It is best to have a bucket of water close to hand for putting out a fire in an emergency.

TIPS AND CONSIDERATIONS

- Collect up some lint from your tumble drier. It takes well to a spark and ignites easily.
- Store bits of silver birch bark, cotton wool, lint and other types of kindling in a waterproof jar in your rucksack.
- Always carry weatherproof matches and/or an artificial flint striker.
- Feather sticks can be made using a piece of dead wood and a sharp knife; they are useful for lighting fires in damp conditions.

COOKING ON A FIRE
Simple foods to cook on a fire:

MARSHMALLOWS A firm favourite with children. Poke marshmallows onto the end of thin sticks and hold them over the embers at the edge of the fire.

CHOC-APPLES Cut off the top of the apple and hollow out the core but don't go right through. Fill the inside with chocolate spread and replace the top of the apple. Tightly wrap the fruit in silver foil then place in the embers for approximately half an hour. Remove carefully using a stick and leave to cool slightly before eating.

BAKED POTATOES Punch some holes into an old biscuit tin. Wrap the potatoes in silver foil and place them in the biscuit tin on top of the embers for 45–50 minutes.

ELLA'S JOKE

Why did the mushroom go to the disco?
—
Because he was a fun guy!

Why did he leave early?
—
Because there wasn't mushroom.

AMY SAYS...

Use a magnifying glass to create a flame — find some old, flakey forest material such as leaves and pile them up (tissue can be used to start the fire as well). Keep your hand very still and hold the magnifying glass over it, so that the sun's rays create a light in the middle of the leafy patch. Then wait till it starts to smoulder. Always make sure the flame is kept under control though.

BUSHCRAFT SURVIVAL SKILLS
SOMETHING FOR NOTHING

Of course you can't ever really get something for nothing, but when you are out in the wild it is possible to make things using only the natural resources around you – and the bushcraft knowledge and skills that you take with you.

A PIECE OF STRING

Once upon a time, all ropes used to be handmade from natural fibres, like hemp. Children can be taught from a young age how to braid and how to make a piece of cordage from nettles, which have strong, thin stems.

Before you start work though, make sure that the children are wearing some decent gloves to protect them from the stinging hairs:

1 Find a tall straight nettle and uproot it.
2 Wearing thick gloves, brush off the stinging hairs and leaves until you are left with a bald stem.
3 Crush the stem between thumb and forefinger and then run your thumbnail down the stem to open it up.
4 Now bend the stem backwards over a finger to cause the inner fibres to break. Remove them, leaving just the outer fibres.
5 Leave the fibres to dry a little before braiding.
6 Fold a length of fibre in half and then roll the fibre separately between your fingers until you get to the end, then let go. The fibres will start to braid themselves. Repeat this step until you feel the piece of cord has been made.

TIPS AND CONSIDERATIONS
- Check to make sure no-one is allergic to nettle stings before you start and have some anti-histamine cream and tablets to hand in case.
- When taking anything from the environment, even nettles, try and consider the impact it will have on its inhabitants.
- When weaving with leaves, make sure to keep the weaving tight.

WEAVING LEAVES

Where thick and rigid leaves are in abundance, you can teach children how to make simple baskets, hats, mats and much more. To get started, pick some native broad grass leaves and weave them using the simple 'under and over' method as follows:

1 Place some leaves horizontally and in parallel.
2 Weave a new blade of grass vertically, going under and over the horizontal leaves.
3 Weave a second leaf, but this time starting by going over and then under.
4 Keep repeating the process until you have a panel of woven leaves.

With this technique mastered, your children can now embark on bigger projects.

DID YOU KNOW?

It is believed that Ancient Egyptians were the first people to create rope and made it out of reed fibres.

ELLA'S JOKE

Three pieces of string went into a bar. The first piece of string went up to the barman and asked, 'Can I have a pint of beer?' The barman replied, 'NO! We don't serve pieces of string at this bar.' So the second piece of string went up to the barman and asked, 'Can I have a pint of beer?' and the barman said 'NO!! We don't serve pieces of string in this bar.' Then the third piece of string went into the toilet, tied himself in a knot, frayed his hair and went back out. He went up to the barman and asked 'Can I have a pint of beer?' and the barman asked 'Are you a piece of string?' The third piece of string replied 'No mate, I'm afraid not!'
[A frayed knot!]

AMY SAYS...

Make a tropical drinks coaster out of wood. Use a pen knife (supervised) to cut it into a circular shape then carve a pattern on it. Finally, place a tropical juice drink on top!

WATCH DEER RUTTING

Watching deer rutting is an exciting autumn spectacle. Whilst it can look brutal, it is a perfectly normal and natural activity that should not be interfered with, but marvelled at.

The deer-rutting season takes place between September and November. During this period, the stags start fighting each other in order to attract and impress female deer and compete for mating rights. They parade around, making strange groaning sounds and lock antlers with any potential threat. The clash of antlers leads to a shoving match in which each male tries to show greater strength. The dominant stag usually gets more females to mate with. Does are only fertile for a short period of time, therefore competition to mate is high.

Deer rutting takes place all over the countryside. It happens in the wild but can more easily be seen in woodlands, parks and country estates. The peak time to appreciate the experience is at dawn and dusk, when the deer are most active. Deer are usually shy, cautious animals that are difficult to spot in the wild. During the rutting season however, stags can be very aggressive and territorial, so therefore it is important to keep a safe distance.

AMY SAYS...

There are many types of deer. So it is certainly a challenge to identify the exact type that you can see. Here are a few types of deer and a description of their appearance so you can pinpoint which species you're watching:

1. **RED DEER** Their summer coat is a reddish brown or brown and their winter coat is grey.

2. **ROE DEER** They have a reddish brown summer coat and a grey, pale brown or, occasionally, black, winter one.

3. **FALLOW DEER** These are the classic 'Bambi' type of deer. They are a tan/fawn colour with white spots on their back in the summer, but are grey with unclear spots in winter.

TIPS AND CONSIDERATIONS

- Wear camouflaged clothing so as not to draw attention to yourself.
- Keep your distance and keep quiet.
- Keep dogs at a safe distance and on a lead.

DID YOU KNOW?

A male deer is called a 'buck' or a 'stag'.

1

2

3

ELLA'S JOKE

What do you get when you
cross Bambi with a ghost?

—

Bamboo.

MOUNTAIN BIKE TRAIL

Complete a challenging bike trail together as a family.

Family cycle challenges can begin as soon as all family members are confident when riding a bike of some kind, and have the strength and stamina to complete their first bike trail.

The main aim behind this challenge is to complete the trail together, so selecting a suitable route is important, and needs to be chosen while bearing in mind the weakest cyclist in your family team. This may be a youngster with a balance bike, or a more senior relative that has been invited along. Collective satisfaction as a group, on completion of the trail, is the reward, so take your time and enjoy the ride.

WHERE TO GO

A sensible starting point for families is to use established trails. Forest or national parks usually have graded and maintained cycle trails. They also have cycle hire and trailer hire, so this challenge really doesn't have an age limit. The routes are usually circular, so you'll make it back to your car (and your picnic) on completion.

More experienced cyclists or those looking for a more 'raw' or extreme challenge might want to head out onto one of the many paths and tracks that can be found in the open countryside. This more adventurous approach requires more pre-trail preparation (route planning) and more of an en-route challenge (map reading, a higher fitness level and bike-handling demands).

TIPS AND CONSIDERATIONS

- No matter what your ability or perceived risk, always wear a helmet. You'll be safer and you'll be modeling safe practice to young riders.
- Encourage young cyclists to be aware of others – the walkers and cyclists ahead of them and, more importantly, an awareness of faster riders behind.
- Carry water, snacks and a simple first aid kit. When venturing further afield, take a puncture repair kit and some bike tools as a minimum.

AMY SAYS...

If there's a skills section, practise bike control as a warm-up and as a way of knowing your bike.

Keep your eyes open for wildlife; you might catch a glimpse in the distance, or get a close-up view if you are quiet (and not puffing too loudly).

A long, strenuous bike ride is a good opportunity to convince your parents that they need to buy you power snacks like chocolate and sweets.

ELLA'S JOKE

Why can a bicycle not stand up on its own?
—
Because it's too tired!

DID YOU KNOW?

Before we started using the word 'bicycle' (from the French 'bicyclette') bicycles were referred to as 'velocipedes'.

NIGHT WALK IN A FOREST

Explore and experience a forest after dark – if you dare!

Darkness brings with it a sense of mystery and excitement. A familiar walk in the street, down a passageway or across a well-trodden park takes on a whole new aura and atmosphere when it's dark – particularly, but not exclusively – for children.

For young children, venturing out into the dark is exhilarating and a little nerve-wracking at the same time. It is exciting because they can carry, and use, their own torch purposefully. It's also nerve-tingling, because the darkness can make things feel, look and sound different. You can ramp up that excitement or scariness factor by taking children on a night walk in a forest. It does not necessarily have to be 'night-time' (since sunset is earlier in the winter) but the important ingredient for this magical experience is darkness.

Initially it may be best to use a familiar location; one that you and the children know well by daylight. It will be enough of a thrill just to be out in the dark with a torch, without needing to be in a new and unfamiliar location as well. This might be a little too unnerving at first, especially for little ones. However, after one or two familiar visits, venture out somewhere previously unexplored for a much more exciting and slightly unsettling experience. You and your children are likely to soon get used to the dark and start to tune into the night-time sounds of the forest. Once you return to the start, there will be a sense of relief, exhilaration and bravery.

TIPS AND CONSIDERATIONS

- Each person should carry a torch or head torch.
- Switch your head torch to a red light setting so that it doesn't affect your night vision.
- Step carefully to avoid tripping up.
- Walk in silence so you can fully appreciate the noises around you.

SHHH!

AMY SAYS...

Turn all the lights off and stand still in the darkness for
two minutes. At first, all you will be able to see is a bright
glow in front of your eyes, but give them time to adjust to
the amount of light there is. Then, just listen and look.
Stay absolutely quiet and observe the forest when night is
nigh. Keep your eyes open for nocturnal animals (creatures
that hunt at night) like hedgehogs and foxes and, if you're
very lucky, maybe even a badger. It's highly likely that you
will see bats as well.

DID YOU KNOW?

A single brown bat can consume
up to 1000 mosquitoes
in a single HOUR!

PEOPLE-FREE WALK

Forests, national parks and other popular family venues often provide trails for exploring an area by foot or by bike. Naturally, if you are new to an area, these seem a sensible option, offering a safe route with a pre-determined distance. But who says you have to follow the path?

Exploring an area by foot can be more exciting if you stay off the paths; avoiding the Tarmac-ed, boarded or gravelled routes and creeping through the natural environment will feel more like an adventure. If the path is covered by sticks, leaves and plants then tread carefully and quietly – who knows what you'll encounter!

If you take along a wildlife book, you can attempt to spot as many different trees, flowers and fungi as possible while you explore. Many children nowadays are often unable to spot and identify native species, so encouraging youngsters to find them outdoors for themselves can be a rewarding natural treasure hunt.

Getting lost is a possibility but you can always play it safe – be aware of where the paths are and follow them from a distance so you know you are never far from one.

For older, more daring children, the route can be kept completely away from any paths. Rather than follow a map, use it for reference only, as a way of tracking where you have been, rather than where you are heading.

AMY SAYS...

HIDE AND SNEAK Walk stealthily to avoid being seen by people walking on nearby paths. Creeping along in the woods or long grass is effective because when a passer-by approaches, you can dart behind a tree or dive into the cover of long reeds or grass. Try to avoid walking along busy bridleways so that an encounter with a person is even more unlikely.

TIPS AND CONSIDERATIONS

- Walk quietly and you might spot some wildlife such as deer, rabbits, lizards etc.
- Wear insect repellent when appropriate to avoid getting bitten or stung by insects.
- Be prepared to possibly get stung by nettles or scratched by the undergrowth.
- Don't pick any unknown plants or fungi – some are poisonous and harmful.
- Take along snacks and drinks if you don't know how long you'll be walking for. It's always a good idea to have food and drinks to keep up your energy levels.

DID YOU KNOW?

In 1990 the UK Countryside Commission reported that 12,000 long-distance walkers and 250,000 day-walkers were using all or part of the Pennine Way per year. Now that's busy!

ELLA'S JOKE

What runs but never walks?

—

Water!

SLACKLINING

Slacklining is a relatively new sport that you may encounter at an outdoor event. You may also happen upon 'slackers' practising. So, what is it? Think of it as tightrope walking on a tensioned strap that is suspended above the ground at a minimum height of 30cm/12in. It is a fun activity for all the family and one in which kids and parents can learn alongside one another. As a sport, it is inclusive for beginners and experts alike, because it is challenging, whatever your level of skill.

The fun begins with trying to balance on the strap – an achievement in itself! Once this is mastered, you can progress to the next skill, which is walking and turning. Eventually you may even be able to perform complicated acrobatic moves.

As a form of exercise, slacklining is surprisingly effective. The act of trying to balance strengthens core muscles and joints. Consequently, the sport is used as a form of rehabilitation for people recovering from back or joint injuries. In addition to the physical benefits, slacklining is also good for developing perseverance and a determined mindset. Many kids these days give up trying something new too easily, but slacklining counters the 'Give up. It's too hard' mentality. Perseverance and concentration lead to simple, rewarding gains, such as balancing or taking two steps, and effort is instantly rewarded.

Where might you be able to try slacklining? The opportunity is most likely to arise at an outdoor event such as an adventure festival or local fête but, if you are really keen, it is easy to purchase one of the many different types of slacklines from various worldwide manufacturers. Slackline kits are small, affordable and lightweight, so are easy to transport anywhere in a small rucksack, along with your picnic. If you do buy a slackline, it will come with set-up instructions that are simple to follow.

This is one time when you'll be pleased to be called a 'slacker'. So go on then, give it a go. No slacking!

TIPS AND CONSIDERATIONS

- Always look straight ahead at the tree or anchor; don't look down!
- Make sure that your feet are pointing along the line; avoid side stepping.
- Use your arms and non-walking leg to provide extra balance.
- Concentrate and block out distractions.
- Ensure that there is plenty of tension in the strap – the tighter the better!

SAFETY

- Choose a safe and appropriate location.
- Start slacklining at a low height.
- Set up above flat ground without bumps or holes that could cause injuries.
- Avoid overloading the line.

AMY SAYS...

Get your parents to set up the slackline (it really is something they need to do), but you can have plenty of fun playing on it. Here are some things to try:

- Start by bouncing up and down on your bottom on the slackline.
- Get three generations balancing together on the slackline — child, parent and grandparent!
- Play 'Who am I?' Strike a pose or perform mannerisms on the slack line. Whoever guesses correctly is the next person to have a go.

ELLA'S JOKE

Why did the lion eat the slackliner?
—
Because she wanted her meal to be well balanced!

DID YOU KNOW?

Slacklining, while being a fun sport in itself, is performed by many sportsmen and sportswomen as rehabilitation after injury, since it builds up and strengthens core muscles.

SLEEP IN A WOOD

What is so adventurous about sleeping in the forest? Nothing... except that the tricks that your imagination may play on you can make this an uncomfortable experience. But adventuring is all about extending your comfort zones and rising to a challenge.

The forest is often regarded as a place of shelter or protection in the daytime or during inclement weather. Most people explore the woods by day, but forests and woods come alive in the dark as they take on a new form; when dusk falls, the forest feels very different – that's when it's time to head off for a family adventure.

Once you've decided how you are going to sleep (bivvi, hammock, tent or under a tarpaulin), find a suitable spot. Stay close to home initially; somewhere you are familiar with, and somewhere you can bail out from, if needs be. Try to find somewhere off the beaten track but reasonably accessible – the deeper you go into the forest, the more exhilarating the experience. Head in an hour before dusk to find a suitable spot.

Remember that the forest will naturally appear darker, cooler and damper than the great outdoors. Expect to use torch lights and be ready to put on extra layers of clothing sooner than you would normally anticipate doing so. Gradually, your eyes will become acclimatized to the levels of darkness. If possible, switch your head torch to a red setting; avoid using white light, as this will cause you to lose your night vision.

When you hear the birds roosting up in the trees, all that remains is to get into your sleeping bag and tune into the night sounds: owl hoots, the rustling of badgers or foxes and the snoring of nearby family members!

Don't worry if you need a pee in the night. There's plenty of lav-a-trees!

TIPS AND CONSIDERATIONS

Remember to respect the environment, as you are only a transient guest. Clear up any litter and leave no trace of your stay.

AMY SAYS...

- Go off and explore while the adults are doing the boring stuff, like setting up. Look for a tree to climb or somewhere to build a den. You could even look for signs of wildlife, such as footprints and animal pooh, or try to track a wild animal.
- Find a wooden staff to help you walk through and beat down nettles and bramble briers.
- Try to identify as many trees as possible in the area around your woodland camp.

ELLA'S JOKE

What do you call a sleeping bull?

—

A bull-dozer!

DID YOU KNOW?

The forest area of the world is about 4 billion hectares, which represents nearly 30% of the Earth's landmass.

SPEND A NIGHT IN A LOG CABIN

Log cabins offer a more luxurious stay away from home than camping. Although relatively tame, they provide an introduction to sleeping away from home comforts, a taste of 'glamping' and a stepping-stone to sleeping out in the wild. It is the environment or location that is important and provides a platform from which you can explore and feel connected with nature; the setting itself feels exciting and different. Since log cabins are often located in the middle of woodland or a forest and in a car-free zone, you feel immersed in nature.

Depending on the location, log cabins vary in comfort, from minimal to luxurious. They may be one of many dwellings within a resort or an individual, isolated building in a remote place. Whichever you choose, your cabin will provide the base from which to try other outdoor activities and whatever the weather, you can always return to a log cabin for warmth and shelter when you are cold, wet, muddy, hungry or tired.

When you get up each morning to see the woodland waking up, start the day with breakfast outdoors. Cook porridge on a gas stove and feed the birds at the same time, by leaving out breadcrumbs or hanging up fat balls. Instead of preparing a regular picnic, how about cooking a one-pot meal instead? In the evening, try barbecuing in the fresh air.

TIPS AND CONSIDERATIONS

- Take your own bikes, as cycle hire will be an added cost. Also consider taking scooters for Tarmac-ed areas.
- If you have a choice of cabin, choose one that's on the periphery away from people, to make it a more wild experience!
- When skiing, consider staying in a log cabin instead of in hotel accommodation. This will be a more rustic alpine experience.

AMY SAYS...

FUN GAME: 1,2,3 HOME (OR 40-40-HOME)

Find somewhere that can be the base and choose a person to be the tagger. That person then closes their eyes and counts to twenty. The other players run to find somewhere to hide. When the time is up, the tagger shouts, 'Ready or not, here I come!' and goes to look for the other hiding players. Meanwhile, the others are trying to run back to base without being caught by the tagger. If they get back to base without being tagged, they shout either, '1,2,3 home!' or '40-40-home' depending on what you call the game. However, if someone is caught, they immediately become the tagger and the old tagger has to run to base.

DID YOU KNOW?

When log cabins were first built, the doors faced south to allow the sun to shine into the cabin during the day.

ELLA'S JOKE

Why do dragons sleep during the day?

—

So they can fight knights!

WALK ON THE HIGH ROPES

High wire trails and ropewalks are becoming increasingly common as national forests become popular tourist venues for walkers, mountain bikers and general outdoor types.

The selection of tunnels, balance beams, Tarzan swings and ziplines, all 9m/30ft above the forest floor, provides an exciting playground for different ages and abilities. You don't have to be super fit to complete the course, but must be able to climb a ladder. A head for heights is beneficial, but those with a fear can be supported, or opt for easier routes.

Due to safety considerations and the equipment required, this activity is best undertaken via a provider so it also comes with a price tag, but your offspring will certainly say afterwards that it was well worth the fee. There are restrictions: children usually have to be aged 10 or over and more than 1.4m/4ft 6in tall. Many junior courses are appearing alongside the more established routes, so younger children do not feel left out and can experience similar levels of exhilaration from completing routes that are appropriate for their size.

When you arrive at your provider they will supply you with the necessary equipment (harness, helmet, ropes and carabineers). The instructors will demonstrate how to use the carabineers safely and how to put everything on.

ELLA'S JOKE

Which type of dinosaur could jump higher than high ropes?
—
Any kind! The high ropes can't jump!

Completing the treetop adventure usually takes 2-3 hours, depending on confidence and ability. Providers are usually set up in picturesque forest locations so you not only get the excitement of the activity but also an appreciation of the environment that you are in. Once you've finished, you can enjoy a picnic or walk through the woods to spot some wildlife.

TIPS AND CONSIDERATIONS

- Wear comfortable clothing.
- Wear comfortable footwear that grips well and won't fall off.
- If scared of heights, keep looking ahead!
- Help younger children to clip on and off.

AMY SAYS...

Don't look down — see who can go the longest without looking downwards.

Be an ape and try to make your movements as smooth as possible. If you want, you could make some noises. Also, If there are steep swings, do the Tarzan call and whack your chest — don't start swinging on vines though!

DID YOU KNOW?

The biggest difference between apes and monkeys is that apes are more intelligent.

WHITTLE WHILE YOU WALK

It might feel counter-intuitive to give a young child a knife but, with the right introduction and appropriate tools, children can be taught to use one safely from a young age. Whittling is a traditional craft that encourages precision, attention to detail and patience. It simply involves carving or shaping an ordinary stick with a knife blade into a creative sculpture or even a useful tool.

SAFETY FIRST

Before kids can start whittling, it is essential to establish some key safety points. Familiarize yourself with knife safety before allowing your child to use a knife. Here are some essential safety tips:

- Always make sure that a child is supervised when using a knife.
- Start with a child-friendly safety knife; this will have a lock on it and a rounded end, instead of a point.
- Demonstrate how to hold the knife safely.
- Teach children to always cut away from the body.
- Only cut when in a static position (sitting down or kneeling).

GETTING STARTED

Begin with an idea of what you want to achieve; this makes learning to whittle more purposeful. Here are a few ideas for budding whittlers:

MAKING A SIMPLE WALKING STICK
Find a stick that is a suitable height, strip off the bark and flatten the knots. Spend extra time smoothing and shaping the handle end for comfort.

MAKING AN ADVANCED WALKING STICK
Once your stick has been made, try to whittle the end into a simple shape. This involves more discipline because it is trying to achieve a definite shape (such as a dog, bird etc.)

MAKE A LITTER PICKER
Sharpen the end of a stick and use it to pick up litter while out on a walk.

AMY SAYS...

If you are make a walking stick why not use it to show off a badge collection? You can often buy souvenir walking stick badges at the different places you visit. Fix them to a sanded and varnished walking stick and you will have your own unique trophy to remind you of the places that you have been.

DID YOU KNOW?

Balsa wood is, for most people, the best wood to whittle with.

ELLA'S JOKE

What's the best way to carve wood?

—

Whittle by whittle!

WATER

Adventures in and around water can be especially exciting and invigorating. Whether you go wild swimming in a lake or clamber into a kayak to travel down a river, there are many family expeditions to be had on water in the great outdoors. Have fun building your own raft, sleeping by a lake, learning to sail or scrambling up a stream while enjoying the fresh air.

BIVVI BY A RIVER

Sleep in a bivvi bag by a river and enjoy looking out for endangered wildlife, such as otters, while you are outdoors.

Spending time by a river is one of the most relaxing things you can do. The sound of a river's constant meandering flow is soothing and calming. Enjoy the peaceful scene, watch flies dance effortlessly on the swirls and ebbs of the currents, disturbed momentarily only by a rising fish.

When you spend time quietly watching and waiting, you have the best chance of seeing some of the shyest river habitants: otters and beavers, or if the season is right, salmon heading back up river to spawn.

Not sounding like an adventure? Well, as the darkness descends and you start setting up your camp, the river environment you have got to know so well takes on a dark and slightly eerie look, and as your night vision is honed, so too is your sense of hearing. Roosting birds and hooting owls will be heard, and the silent swooping bats will be silhouetted against the backdrop of dusk.

Sleep close to the river and be lulled to sleep by its rhythmic sounds – ones you can only hear when the background noise of daytime is hushed. Whether you hammock, bivvi or camp in a tent, a night by a river is so rewarding, and well worth a try.

AMY SAYS...

Make friends with a bat. As dusk descends, look out for bats feeding on moths as well as other flying insects that come out at night. When an unsuspecting bat flies by, throw a small stone up in the air but don't aim for the bat. If timed correctly, the bat will swoop close by until it realizes the stone you threw is not a tasty, flying critter. Don't worry about hitting the bat with the stone; it is more likely to hit you if you aren't watching out for it!

Using riverside vegetation, make a den to sit in (and maybe hide in) and watch for creatures of the river — and I don't mean flies. Try to spot a kingfisher or a fish jumping out of the water to catch a fly. If you sit still and quietly, it's amazing what you'll see!

Big, thick-leaved reeds are great for making a natural whistle. Pick a leaf and make a thin slit with your thumbnail in the centre — ideally on the vein. Trap the leaf between your thumbs and blow hard. Experiment with how you hold the leaf until you achieve a high-pitched squeal (OK, it won't be quite a whistle).

ELLA'S JOKE

Where do fish wash?

—

In a river basin!

DID YOU KNOW?

The longest river in Great Britain is the Severn, measuring 345km/214 miles) long!

BUILD A BRIDGE

Find a stream or a river and use nearby natural materials for building.

Bridges come in all shapes and sizes but the aim of this family adventure is to simply use natural materials to form a structure that provides a route – dry if possible – from one side of a small ditch or stream to the other. The structure needs to act as a bridge for the whole family to cross, once completed.

Part of the fun is finding the expanse that you wish to span with your bridge; this could be in the woods or in the nearby countryside. The next important job is to find suitable materials with which to build. A woodland location is ideal, because you can often find broken branches and wooden debris to collect and drag to the water's edge to use. It's important to discourage young bridge builders from disturbing or damaging the living environment though.

Teamwork is important and assigning roles helps the process work more smoothly; some of the family members can be in charge of finding and collecting materials while one or two stay in situ to construct it. You don't

have to be a structural engineer for this (but it helps!).

This task can be completed in all weathers, but allow plenty of time, and keep warm.

EQUIPMENT NEEDED

- Gloves for handling branches and spiky materials.
- Pen knife and/or small saw.
- A first aid kit, just in case.

TIPS AND CONSIDERATIONS

- Know your limits. Don't pick up anything that is too heavy.
- Wear gloves to protect your hands.
- Do not disturb nature.

ELLA'S JOKE

Three men are trapped on an island. They find a genie's lamp and each gets a wish. The first man wishes he was 25% smarter, then swims off the island. The second man wishes he was 50% smarter then cuts down a tree, makes a boat and rows off the island. The third man wishes he was 100% smarter then he walks across the bridge!

AMY SAYS...

Play 'The Last Word' — a simple game for two or more bridge builders to play. Take turns saying any word with the word 'bridge' in it. Avoid repetitions. The winner is the person that has the last word.

EXAMPLES:
- 'Humber Bridge' (a large suspension bridge spanning the River Humber in the UK)
- 'Stamford Bridge' (Chelsea Football Club's ground in London)
- 'Beau Bridges' (a movie actor)

DID YOU KNOW?

- The simplest type of bridge is a beam bridge that is supported by both banks.
- Bridges must be built strong enough to safely support their own weight as well as the weight of whatever is going to travel over them.

CANOE DOWN A RIVER

A canoe, not to be confused with a kayak, which has an enclosed cockpit and is a smaller vessel, can comfortably accommodate up to four people and is therefore a natural choice of transport for a family seeking to explore a river. Canoes are relatively stable and easy to control, while being roomy enough to allow you to carry a certain amount of luggage and essentials with you.

Beginner families should look to hire a canoe from a provider who can supply the vessel, paddles and buoyancy aids – a must for children and non-swimmers. The provider can also advise on the best places for paddling. Providers are usually based on or near rivers, so hiring your equipment also solves the issue of 'how do I transport the canoe to the river?'.

Once you've got two or three river trips under your buoyancy aid belt, you're likely to want to 'go it alone'. Hiring equipment can be expensive, but again, it saves you having to transport equipment yourself, as providers usually offer a drop-off and collection service. You might not even have to buy or hire at all; ask around friends and family, and you might find one who will lend you a canoe for free.

WHAT TO TAKE

- Life jackets – don't just take them with you, remember to wear them.
- First aid kit – drop in some insect repellent or sting cream for good measure.
- Water and snacks – hungry paddlers are not happy paddlers so keep everyone fuelled up.

TIPS AND CONSIDERATIONS

- Planning a trip – remember that, unless you are on a tidal river, the water only flows in one direction. It's advisable for families new to canoeing to try the up-stream leg first. If your paddlers get tired, at least you can then drift downstream towards your exit point.
- It you're in a big group, or want to do longer trips requiring more provisions, tie or 'raft' two canoes together.

CANOE LIMERICK

There was a young man from Crewe
Who wanted to build a canoe
When he got to the river
He found with a shiver
He hadn't used waterproof glue!

AMY SAYS...

Sing a song to sing to take your mind off the effort of paddling:

- 'Row, row, row your boat' (or 'paddle, paddle, paddle your canoe').
- Viking/Dragon boat chants: 'Heave ho, yo oh, heave ho...'
- Nemo theme: 'Keep on paddling'.

KEEP QUIET AND PADDLE ON As the name
suggests, the aim is to keep quiet. You may spot some river
wildlife going about their daily business. If you're lucky, you
may see not just midges, but a kingfisher. Fish are also
common in rivers so you are likely to see varieties of them
(don't count on seeing clownfish or sharks though!)

DID YOU KNOW?

The River Thames used to
be clogged up with muck
because the sewers ran into
it. In Parliament they had to
hold handkerchiefs to their
noses to block out the smell.

CROSS A SUSPENSION BRIDGE

Walk across the longest suspension bridge you can find, then come back again.

Ever since the dawn of civilization, humans have had to build bridges to span rivers and bodies of water, to connect important roads. For this reason, there is something innately pleasing about seeing and traversing a bridge.

Suspension bridges have added appeal due to their architectural design and often iconic status. Walking across a suspension bridge brings you literally in touching distance with the nuts and bolts that hold the whole structure together. With bolt heads the size of a young child, you get a sense of the enormous scale of the bridge and the feat of engineering brilliance responsible for its design and build.

The longer suspension bridges enable you to see the effects of curvature of the Earth; a source of fascination, intrigue – and disbelief – for youngsters.

TIPS AND CONSIDERATIONS

- Charity events are usually organized around local suspension bridges. These may be sponsored walks or bike rides. Look out in your local papers for the next event and consider joining in.
- Do some research about famous suspension bridges around the world; this will provide conversation during your walk.

AMY SAYS...

NUMBER PLATE GAME There'll be lots of cars and trucks passing you on the bridge. Each time one passes by, look at the number plate and use the last three letters to make up a silly phrase or sentence. Examples include:

STA Strawberries taste awesome.
DEG Don't eat grass.

There are loads of nuts and bolts holding the suspension bridge together. See how many you can count as you're walking along. Try not to count the same one twice!

When you reach the middle of the bridge, look over the edge and see how high you are above the water. Try out some science — how long will it take two different-sized objects to fall to the water below? Will it take the same time or not? Choose small objects like pieces of gravel. NEVER throw anything if there is something below the bridge that it could hit.

ELLA'S JOKE

What did the
Humber Bridge say
to the cars crossing it?

—

*The suspense
is killing me!*

DID YOU KNOW?

The longest suspension bridge in the world is Akashi Kaikyo in Japan and is 1991m/2177yds long.

DAM A STREAM

Stopping or redirecting the flow of a stream is harder than it sounds.

Stemming the flow of water in a stream is in some respects the ultimate challenge; very difficult to complete, better attempted as a team, and one that requires great determination and perseverance. It's also 'dam' good fun.

Find a stream and then walk against the flow until you find a section that you want to try and dam. You will need a good supply of stones and pebbles close by, plus green vegetation for plugging small gaps. Unless you want to try to dam the whole stream, find a natural pool that has only one or two flowing outlets – these are what you will need to block off.

This activity is guaranteed to get the whole family involved, as adults will find it hard to just sit back and watch. Interestingly you'll find that different people take on different roles: stone finders, carriers, dam builders, structural engineers etc. Dam building provides a good opportunity for youngsters to become aware of what constitutes effective team-work. It also helps them to realize the importance of combining the skills and talents of individuals when working collaboratively on a project that has a shared and definite goal.

TIPS AND CONSIDERATIONS

- Take a picnic – dam building is hungry and thirsty work, and it would be a shame not to take advantage of an opportunity to eat al fresco, in a spectacular outdoor location.
- Take 'before and after' photographs of your damming effort. If there is a noticeable difference between the two photos, you have done well.

AMY SAYS...

Take some toy boats (or make your own) to play with in the rapids and also in the pool created by your dam. Make sure that they aren't precious to you or damaging to the environment in case they happen to drift out of the pool and downstream, out of your reach!

WHITE-WATER POOH-STICK RACING Take Pooh-stick racing to a new level. Start the race up stream and make a funny commentary of the stick racing down the river. It may even end up in your dam, which could be the finish.

DAM BUSTERS Just before you leave, stand within throwing distance of your manmade wall (out of the way of people of course) and blast your dam to pieces by throwing rocks and boulder to let the natural flow of the stream start again.

DID YOU KNOW?

In World War Two, a bouncing bomb was created by Sir Barnes Wallis and was used by the Royal Air Force to attack dams in the Ruhr Valley, Germany.

ELLA'S JOKE

What did the fish say when it swam into a wall?

—

Dam!

FLOAT DOWN A RIVER

Go with the flow and let the river take you downstream, without a boat.

Why rely on a kayak, canoe or raft to travel down a river when you could float sedately downstream at a river's natural pace? You will literally be going with the flow. This simple, but fun, activity requires little equipment and costs little, but careful planning is needed to find a suitable river.

Flowing water in rivers and waterfalls stays cold all year round, so to enjoy this adventure you should probably wear wetsuits (shorty or full winter steamer versions). A buoyancy aid, either borrowed or hired, is a must, particularly for less confident swimmers. To protect your feet from the uneven and possibly sharp edges of the riverbed, remember to wear a pair of old trainers or specially designed wet shoes. The chances are, your feet will be sticking out of the water in front of you for a lot of the time, as you float on your back in the direction of the flow. This is the most comfortable position to be in!

Find a suitable entry point that allows everyone to walk into the river and adjust to the water temperature at their own pace. Jumping in unprepared will be a shock to the body and not the best way to start! Then, it's simple – just float and let the current take you downstream. If you come across any small rapids on your way downstream, walk around them or cross your arms, lie back and ride down them. It's really exhilarating riding down your own natural water flume.

TIPS AND CONSIDERATIONS

- Find a river that has a gentle flow, and is suitable for the ability of your swimmers – avoid fast flowing rivers, rapids or large waterfalls!
- Plan suitable points at which to enter and exit the river – you can always choose a short stretch and keep repeating the route.

AMY SAYS...

DRIFTING TAG Make this simple game seem harder by playing it while you are floating with the current. Try and swim away from the tagger, and try to stay behind them so that they have to swim upstream to get you. Always make sure you're looking at what's ahead though, just so you don't run in to any unexpected rapids or miss your exit point.

WATER STATUES Try to create funny shapes and positions in the water while drifting with the flow. Be creative; make as many different positions as possible, like karate or ballerina shapes. Make sure there are no hanging branches in the way when you do the position.

DID YOU KNOW?

The River Danube is Europe's deepest river and is up to 177m/193yds in depth!

ELLA'S JOKE

What do you call the little rivers that flow into the Nile?

—

Juve-Niles!

SLEEP BY A LAKE

Lakes conjure up serene and beautiful images and therefore seem a natural setting in which to set up camp for the night. Why stay in a hotel or a bed & breakfast with a lakeside view when you could pitch your tent at the lakeside itself for a fraction of the cost? You wake up to a view of natural beauty, and you don't have to look at it through a window. This is certainly a more adventurous choice for a family night away from home!

Spend the day exploring the edges of the lake by foot or by bike, or get out onto the water in a canoe, kayak or standup paddle board. Then as evening draws in, find a spot to bed down for the night. This could vary from a pebbly beach to a grassy bank. Cook a simple meal on a gas stove or on a campfire and then snuggle down in your sleeping bags. Whether camping in tents, hammocks or bivvi bags, try to watch the sunset and the stars reflected in the water (as long as it's a clear night), while listening to the birdlife chirping their goodnights.

In the morning, after a breakfast in the fresh air, you're already on location for more exploring. If you're feeling brave enough, why not freshen up with a dip in the water?

TIPS AND CONSIDERATIONS

- Choose a sheltered spot that is, ideally, exposed to the sun but not the wind. If you have a lot to carry, camp near to your vehicle.
- Pack lightly. Think carefully about what you'll need to take. You'll have to carry everything so check if you really need each item you've packed.
- Take a camping stove, food and drink. It's always good to go to sleep on a full stomach then have a hearty breakfast in the outdoors.
- Take layers to wear in the evening when the temperatures drop.

AMY SAYS...

SKIMMING STONES This is a really simple activity to do when you're on the banks of a lake. All you need are a few flat, smooth stones and a long stretch of water.

Try to skim the stone along the top of the water so that it bounces forward a few times.

A good technique is to turn sideways with your throwing arm away from the water and your opposite shoulder facing the water. Bring your arm quite far back and then bring it forward with speed, but flat. Oh, and let go of the stone! Make sure that you're quite close to the water if you want to skim properly.

Why don't you try different styles and sizes of stones and see which ones skim the best? Have a competition to see who can skim the most.

ELLA'S JOKE

Why did the teacher jump into the lake?

—

Because she wanted to test the waters!

DID YOU KNOW?

The deepest lake in the world is Lake Baikal in Siberia, Russia. It is 1741m deep — that's more than a mile!

KAYAKING

Hire or borrow kayaks, then go and explore a lake.

Kayaks tend to be single-person vessels – although two-person varieties are also available. Hiring your kit is the best way to try this activity so that you get the right equipment from the start. You will need a wetsuit and a buoyancy aid, as well as a safe location for kayaking that offers safety boat cover. Those new to the sport may also consider taking a beginner lesson.

When you first find yourself in the cockpit of a kayak, try to master some of the basics. Hold the paddle properly – arms shoulder-width apart with knuckles facing upwards. Lean forward slightly and dig the paddle in, then pull it backwards until it is level with your body. To get extra power and efficiency, straighten your non-pulling arm in a punching action, effectively 'pushing' it away from you. This will help you to use different muscles and delay the tired feeling you can get in your arms.

Once you can paddle in a straight line, practise turning; this can be achieved by making a wider pulling stroke, and/or performing a small backwards paddling action with the non-pulling arm.

Now you are ready to enjoy the freedom of being on your own in a single-seater kayak, on the open water, it's time to explore any lake islands, islets and beaches that may be within reach.

TIPS AND CONSIDERATIONS

- Make sure well-fitting buoyancy aids are always worn.
- Keep young paddlers warm as they will soon get fed up if they are cold.

DID YOU KNOW?

In 2010 a kayaker called Tyler Bradt successfully went over Washington's Palouse Falls (56.6m/62yds), gaining a new kayak waterfall world record.

AMY SAYS...

Some favourite playground games can be easily adapted for the water:

- **DOBBIE** (or bob-ie perhaps) Whoever is 'on' or 'it' has to 'dob' a canoe with their paddle. The kayaker that is dobbed becomes 'it'.
- **BULLDOG** This classic playground game works well when you have a large group of paddlers. Perhaps a better name for this is Bullfrog!
- **KAYAK FOOTBALL** Throw a football into the water and flick it around with your paddle towards your opponent's goal. NB. Expect lots of dribbling!

ELLA'S JOKE

Knock Knock
Who's there?
Canoe
Canoe who?
Canoe tell me some good kayak jokes?

KAYAK SAFARI

Exploring the coast by sea kayak really feels like an adventure. You are out on your own, exposed and vulnerable to the might and power of the ocean, guided only by the wind, waves and tides.

Heading out and away from the shallows of a beach or pontoon can feel a little bit intimidating to young paddlers – and probably for many adult paddlers too. The colour of the sea becomes darker as it gets deeper, and your imagination may conjure up threatening imagery (usually containing a shark or two). Reassure frightened paddlers; the fear usually fades quite quickly.

Inexperienced kayaking families will find 'sit on' kayaks the best place to start. They offer good stability and with the lack of a cockpit to sit in, remove the risk of a paddler being trapped inside a capsized sea kayak. The downside is that they sit higher in the water and can be difficult to steer when it is windy. Two-person sit-on kayaks are ideal for families with young children.

'Proper' sea kayaks sit lower in the water and are generally easier to steer and control. They are narrower and contain cockpits, so some degree of paddler competence and experience is required. Once you are out on the water, paddle out and begin to explore

the coastline, looking for birds and sea-life, as well as interesting geographical features such as interesting cliffs, secluded beaches, hidden caves and curious stacks.

TIPS AND CONSIDERATIONS

- Before you venture out, make sure you tell someone where you are going and what time you expect to be back.
- Make sure you know the movements of the tide on the day you decide to safari.
- Don't paddle too near to over-hanging sea cliffs, or cliffs that appear to have loose material.
- Don't venture too deep into sea caves, particularly if there is a significant amount of swell.
- Wear buoyancy aids at all times.
- Apply sun cream regularly.

AMY SAYS...

Take masks, snorkels and fins on the off-chance that you decide to plop over the side to explore what is under the water.

If the conditions are right – and you are paddling with an adult – have a go at rock hopping. To do this, look for a place where the swell can take you and deposit you on a flat rock area. Sit there and wait for the next swell, then paddle like mad to escape.

ELLA'S JOKE

Two kayakers are paddling out at sea.
The waves start to get bigger. One
turns to the other and says, 'If the
kayak tips over, will we fall out?' 'No!'
replies the other, 'We'll still be friends!'

DID YOU KNOW?

The record for the most kayaks and
canoes rafted together was made in
2011 and comprised 1902 boats.

MAKE A **ROPE SWING**

Attach some rope to a branch near a river or lake, then swing over and into the water.

Today's generation of children are spending less time outdoors and missing out on fun activities that children in the past often enjoyed. Playing on a rope swing is a perfect example of this.

Trees beside a river are obvious locations for building a rope swing. The entrance in and out of the water is also an important factor; find a suitably flat spot that allows easy and safe access in and out. A river beach is a an ideal place.

It is best to use your own rope rather than to trust an existing rope. Use a car tow-line or a static rope and choose a healthy, living, thick branch (appropriate for your weight) over which to loop it. Once you've looped the rope over the branch, tie the two ends together (this method allows you to take the rope home with you at the end). Experiment with different ways to create a seat and a handle knot. A short stick for a seat makes it easier for younger children to stay on. Spend time making sure the rope is secure and stress-test it with the heaviest adult before starting.

TIPS AND CONSIDERATIONS

- Be wary of using an existing rope swing – make a sensible decision on how old and safe it looks.
- Check for rocks in the water.
- Check the trajectory of the swing because it will vary depending on the start position in relation to the anchor – the last thing you want is to leave an imprint of your face in the tree!

DID YOU KNOW?

The origins of rope are unknown but some of the first people to develop tools for making rope were the Ancient Egyptians.

Everyone in the family will have a different technique on the rope swing, so why not celebrate this and turn it into a competition.

AMY SAYS...

IDEAS FOR POSSIBLE ROPE SWING CHALLENGES

Who can stay on the longest?
Who can do the silliest entry into the water?
Who can make the biggest splash?
Who can make the loudest Tarzan noise?
Who can catch a fish with their toes?

Here is another activity that you could do by the river, while waiting for your turn:

WILDLIFE WATCHING Look out for kingfishers, herons and inquisitive fish (if you haven't scared them all away with your Tarzan impressions!).

ELLA'S JOKE

What does Tarzan say when he sees a herd of elephants running towards him?
—
Gulp.

What does Tarzan say when he sees a herd of elephants with sunglasses running towards him?
—
Nothing. He doesn't recognize them.

RAFT BUILDING

Build your own raft and test how good it is by sailing off in it.

The likelihood of having to build a raft in your everyday life is probably quite rare, but it can be great fun learning. Achieving good results is quite difficult, so a bit of planning would be a great idea, and be willing to accept any offers of help too!

Building a raft requires a range of equipment and skills: you ideally need flotation vessels such as large plastic barrels, wooden poles and plenty of rope. There are no set rules about how to build a raft so you can be creative with the equipment that you have, and ask other raft builders for advice.

RAFT ADVICE

If you don't have access to plastic barrels and poles, borrow some from a local scout group.

This is a great family activity – the more the better – since teamwork is definitely needed. Everyone can get involved in jobs such as tying knots or holding poles in place.

Once you've made the raft, you must test how successful it is. The raft should be built close to the water so that it doesn't have to be carried far.

The number of rafters you need will depend on how big a raft you build, but you can always challenge yourselves to see how many people can fit on. Don't forget the paddles!

AMY SAYS...

MINI RAFT BUILDING   Create tiny
rafts out of materials like string, twigs and
bottles. Use the same skills and knots as on
the life-size raft to make it extra secure
(square lashings and 'round turn and two half
hitches'). If you make the raft well and
securely, it should be just as strong as the
proper one (it wouldn't be the best idea to try
and ride on it though!).

TIPS AND CONSIDERATIONS

- You don't need to be an expert at tying
  knots but a handy one to know is a
  'round turn and two half hitches'. You'll
  also have to use square lashings to attach
  poles to each other.
- Have different lengths of rope already cut.
- Use uncoated rope because it tightens
  when wet.
- Have pre-cut sections of 2–3m (2–3yds)
  wooden poles.
- Have tools like pen knives and saws to
  hand, if needed.

DID YOU KNOW?

The highest commercially rafted waterfall in the
world is the 7m/7.5 yds-high Tutea falls. It is
part of the Kaituna River, New Zealand.

SOURCE TO MOUTH

Travel the length of a river from its start to its finish.

There are hundreds of river walks out there. This challenge starts at the very beginning (a very good place to start!) and follows the length of a river in its entirety; you need to find the source of the river (or spring, lake or reservoir) and follow it until it reaches the mouth (where it joins another larger river) or the end of its course (the sea). Spend some time locating this on a map and planning routes. This might seem like a daunting task but there are plenty of short rivers you could choose.

The advantage of meandering along the riverbank from the source means that you are going with the flow, therefore the gradient is in your favour. As you are walking along the river there should be plenty to spot, such as other tributaries, bends, waterfalls or weirs. There are plenty of discussions to be had about the flow of the water and the widening of the river as the water volume increases.

This is a family adventure in which you can bank on having a good time!

RIVER VOCABULARY

Don't forget to look up this list of river vocab before you go:
Tributary, meander, beach, bank, erosion, eddy, weir.

TIPS AND CONSIDERATIONS

- You might not have to go far to find the source of a stream or river; look in your local area for springs or lakes.
- Start small, maybe locally, and find a short river to follow from source to mouth then build up to following longer rivers. For a greater challenge, follow a river from its source to the sea.
- Do it in stages – walk sections of a river on several different occasions.
- Always follow the country code and respect the environment that you are in.
- You don't have to walk this challenge (although you could do so at the source) – Instead why not cycle it or canoe, kayak or raft your way along the river's edge?

AMY SAYS...

Practise your rhyming skills
with this scouting song
At the Quartermaster's Stores

There are snakes, snakes, snakes,
Big as garden rakes,
At the store! At the store!
There are snakes, snakes, snakes,
Big as garden rakes, at the
Quartermaster's store.

Substitute other rhyming words
such as 'bears, but no one really
cares' or 'mice running through
the rice'.

ELLA'S JOKE

What did the sea say to the river?
—
You've got such a big mouth!

STREAM SCRAMBLING

Take a more exciting route up a gorge.

Scrambling up a stream valley feels like a really rugged adventure that offers challenge, risk and usually stunning views that get better the higher you climb.

The idea is to simply find a mountain or hill stream and walk against the flow towards its upland source, sticking as close as you can to the water at all times. The lower, flatter sections will be gentle and relaxing, but as the journey progresses, the scramble over rocks and boulders will become more challenging and exhilarating.

As with most family adventures, as long as there are no specific time restrictions, don't rush; take your time and look back regularly to take in the views. A casual pace will ensure careful foot placement and reduce the chance of unwanted trips and falls.

This adventure activity, by its very nature, involves some danger and risk – obviously the more difficult the route, such as a steep gradient, rocky or slippery terrain, the greater the risk. For this reason, if you are taking young adventurers out stream scrambling, it is sensible to do a 'recce' beforehand to ensure the level of challenge is appropriate.

Any successful scrambles you complete can be revisited when the conditions are cold and snowy. The difficulty level will be 'upped' of course, so bear that in mind, but so too will the sense of achievement and reward.

TIPS AND CONSIDERATIONS

- Ensure all scramblers have sturdy and supportive footwear, ideally boots.
- Plan your route carefully beforehand using a suitable map. Use the internet to research proposed routes.
- Turn back if you feel the difficulty level is beyond the weakest member of the group.
- Always have a suitable map with you in case you have to abort the challenge and find an alternative route.
- 'Spot' youngsters on steep sections (this involves standing behind them with arms outstretched in the air ready to provide assistance should a slip or fall occur).

AMY SAYS...

When you're out scrambling you may get so tired that you need a rest. Take some minutes then to dam the stream. Use twigs and other strong materials to block the water, then try to cover up any cracks — otherwise the water may seep through and carry on its way through the stream.

Look for rocks that are shaped like people, animals or things. Let your imagination go wild. You may be surprised how many rocks take on the shape of different animals or things! It may also depend on how you look at the rock — sometimes it looks different depending on the angle at which you view it.

DID YOU KNOW?

Stream scrambling is often called other names such as gorge walking or canyoning.

STAND-UP PADDLEBOARDING

Stand on a board and paddle yourself along a stretch of water.

Stand Up Paddling (SUP) is a relatively new sport, invented in Hawaii by surfers who wanted to be able to paddle out further into the ocean than is possible on a regular surfboard. Now a popular pastime on lakes, rivers and calm coastlines, it is an excellent form of outdoor exercise, particularly as paddling in the standing position develops and tones all of the main muscle groups.

SUP is well suited to families looking to try something new, for one main reason: the boards are very generously proportioned, making them highly stable and therefore able to carry more than one person. This makes SUP accessible for families with small children who are keen to adventure, but not physically big enough to paddle themselves.

Similar to most other water-based activities, hiring equipment from a provider is a good place to start, and hire charges are usually very reasonable. It is also a good idea to SUP on inland water before heading out into the sea and catching a breaking wave. Hiring equipment from a provider will also give the reassurance of safety cover and the option of a tow back into shore if any of your young SUP dudes start to feel chilly.

If you decide to buy your own SUP board, inflatable boards are good value and can be easily packed into a carry bag for easy transportation. The downside is that they are not quite as rigid as other SUP boards, but this shouldn't really be a problem for novice paddlers.

TIPS AND CONSIDERATIONS

- Young paddlers and poor swimmers must always wear buoyancy aids.
- Unless you are in really hot climates, a wetsuit is a must.
- Make sure your SUP board has a leash – so your board doesn't drift off if (and when) you fall in.

AMY SAYS...

To make this an even more fun activity, and if you're
up for getting wet, try some of these mini challenges
on the board:

- Swap boards with someone — you're more likely
  to be wobbled off during this activity when
  you are swapping!
- Do a headstand on the board — if you can do a
  headstand, that is! It's hard to do one!
- See how many people can fit on a board.
- Play dodgems — this is all about paddle power!
- Dance on the board (standing up) — the Macarena
  is a popular choice!

ELLA'S JOKE

What's the worst vegetable
to serve on a paddle board?
—
Leeks!

DID YOU KNOW?

The greatest distance covered on
a stand-up paddle board in 24
hours is 146km (90 miles).

TRY SAILING

Learning to sail as a family may sound quite challenging as it is not as easily accessible as other water sports. It is often associated with big costs, but it can be a fun and fulfilling family experience – something that can grow into a hobby in which the whole family can get involved. It needn't necessarily have to cost the earth either.

There are different ways to try sailing without too much financial commitment. Most sailing clubs offer 'have a go' taster sessions, so you don't have to be experienced, own a boat or even a buoyancy aid – clubs will provide all the necessary equipment and tuition. Alternatively, you might find courses when visiting lakes or seaside locations (at home or abroad). Or you might be lucky enough to know friends or family members who own a boat and can offer you the opportunity to have a go.

Boats come in all shapes and sizes (just like the sailors in them!). When selecting a boat, the size determines how many members will form the crew; a Topper, Optimist or Fun boat is ideal for two youngsters, whereas a dingy will provide ample space for a family.

Spending time together in a boat as a family can be very rewarding. Teamwork, problem solving and communication skills are all needed to become successful at steering the boat and youngsters will also develop a useful awareness of weather conditions.

AMY SAYS...

In the book *Swallows and Amazons* by Arthur Ransome, four children go sailing around Lake Coniston in the Lake District by themselves. They camp on 'Wild Cat Island', aka Peel Island, and explore it with their boat Swallow. They meet two other sailors called the Amazons. Name your boat and sail around a local lake or river then act out what happened in the story (it'll help if you've read the actual book).

Draw a map of the water source that you're sailing on. If you see any islands or coves, give them creative names and if you make the map easy to understand, you could mark a treasure hunt route on it so that others could follow it.

ELLA'S JOKE

Two waves had a race. Who won?

—

They tide!

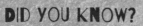

DID YOU KNOW?

Sailors don't use left and right when talking about a boat. They say 'port' for left and 'starboard' for right.

WILD SWIMMING

Many people have been wild swimming without even knowing it; when you go to the beach and swim in the sea, you are, technically, swimming wild. This adventure encourages you to explore different locations and tie in a wild swim with a walk or a campout. What could be more invigorating than a refreshing swim after a long hike or starting the day with a morning swim after sleeping out under the stars?

Unlike swimming pools that are often rectangular, chemical-filled vessels renowned for breeding germs, open water is natural, unpredictable and exhilarating. Swimming pools are, let's face it, not the most picturesque of places, whereas a meandering river in the middle of the countryside or a scenic hillside lake provides a stimulating environment for fun-filled family adventure. In addition to swimming in rivers and lakes, you could also add some excitement by swimming down rapids, under waterfalls, through sea caves or gorges, but remember to only swim where it is safe and suitable for those taking part.

Open-water swimming is often linked with triathlons and many clubs offer novice open-water sessions; this could be an option for first-timers. Some watersports providers also offer guided wild swimming sessions, including the hire of wetsuits and the local knowledge and experience of suitable locations. If confident enough to take the plunge on your own, remember to assess the location carefully to ensure that it is suitable for all participants.

Expect the temperature of open water to be dramatically colder than the water in your local swimming pool! It may be refreshing on a hot day to take a dip in a river or a lake, but if swimming for a longer time, wetsuits are advisable.

TIPS AND CONSIDERATIONS

- Choose locations that have easy entry and exit points.
- Insist that young swimmers and weak swimmers wear buoyancy aids and are accompanied throughout.
- Assess for, and avoid, any dangers such as weeds, strong currents or sharp rocks. If unsure, don't risk it!
- Have snacks and warm drinks handy for when tired swimmers return to shore.

AMY SAYS...

Remember to keep warm and have fun — when you've had enough, come out of the water before you get too cold. Once you are cold, it's hard to get warm again. Try and set yourself a benchmark (for example 'swim to the other side and back before getting out') so that the swim isn't pointless, or too short.

BULLDOG Try and swim to the other side without being tagged by the tagger. If you're caught, join the tagger and try to catch people.

SYNCHRONIZED SWIMMING Get everyone to do a series of dance moves at the same time in the water. If you're ALL up for the challenge, dive underwater and do some moves there too, all at the same time.

DID YOU KNOW?

Elephants can swim as many as 20m/32km per day and use their trunks for snorkels!

ELLA'S JOKE

What kind of swimming stroke can you use on toast?
—
BUTTER-fly!

CLOSE TO HOME

It's perfectly possible to enjoy a number of great adventures in your local area, not far from your front door. Whether you are celebrating your birthday outside, undertaking a few eco-challenges such as going without electricity for a day, or helping the community by clearing up your local park, you will gain a good deal of satisfaction from completing some community challenges, including charity bike rides, that don't take you too far from home.

BIRTHDAY OUTDOORS

Play party games and eat and sleep outdoors, with friends and family.

A children's birthday party held outdoors is much more exciting than a traditional house-based sleepover. In fact, once a child has enjoyed an outdoor celebration, the chances are they will never want an indoor party again.

Erect a decent-sized tent and then let the 'rabble' sort out bedding. This could take them all of five seconds or five hours, after which they'll immediately want to head outside to explore or play.

Rather than providing traditional party food, encourage the children to do some cooking. Supervising children to cook their own food adds enjoyment for them and entertainment for the adults. It's surprising how many children are not accustomed to cooking anything themselves. Get them to cook (or perhaps burn) their own hotdogs and burgers over a disposable BBQ, accompanied perhaps by some grilled sweetcorn cobs or vegetable kebabs. Follow this by toasting marshmallows on twigs that they 'forage' around the campsite. Keep the food arrangements simple; there's no need to dilute the fun by trying to complicate the cooking experience.

After another session of games, heat up some hot chocolate before getting the campers to bed down for the night. Don't worry if they don't brush their teeth on this occasion – after all, it is an adventure!

Oh, and remember to sing *Happy Birthday* some time before lights out.

TIPS AND CONSIDERATIONS

- Take a bag of play equipment for some classic campsite games. Challenge the party group to invent a new game using any of the equipment.
- Make sure the campers know what to do in the night if they need the toilet or are unhappy. Avoid them wandering around to the toilet block on their own – they can go in pairs or with an adult.
- Monitor the cooking of meat products to avoid poorly tummies.

AMY SAYS...

Make the tent an adult-free zone; it's loads more fun without any oldies telling you to do this or that. The tent should be your territory and any intruders who step foot on your ground face serious consequences!

Ask other children at the campsite to join in; team games like rounders work best when there are loads of players on each team. They may appreciate you going up to them and asking them if they want to play, as they may have been too shy to ask you.

Night-time games are really exciting — hide and seek in the dark is thrilling (and sometimes a little bit creepy) especially if your campsite is near a wood. Be careful not to get lost. Take a torch and don't go too far away without anyone else or adult supervision.

Midnight feasts are great when camping. They can consist of any food you like, and don't have to be at midnight.

ELLA'S JOKE

What did one candle say to the other?
—
'Don't birthdays burn you out?'

DID YOU KNOW?

Thousands of people camp at the Glastonbury music festival each year — what a party!

CHARITY BIKE RIDE

Cycling is a great family activity and a popular sport in many countries. If most family members have a bike, then getting outdoors and covering some miles together can be rewarding. However, it will be even more rewarding if the cycling is not only for you, but a charity of your choice.

There are many bike ride options, for both beginners and experts, ranging from fun rides to competitive fast races and epic treks. Choose an event that is most appropriate for your abilities, but try and opt for something that will be a challenge at the same time. Charity events are held all over the country throughout the year. A simple search will soon inform you of a local event and which charity

it is in aid of. It doesn't have to be local; you could go further afield and visit a different area – what better way to appreciate a new city or the countryside than on a bike?

Alternatively you could create your own charity cycle ride. Simply decide a date, mileage and a route that you can realistically achieve. Once you've chosen your charity, collect donations and raise awareness with one of the many fundraising websites. Then you have only to complete the challenge.

TIPS AND CONSIDERATIONS

- Wear comfortable clothing, footwear and a helmet.
- Choose a distance that is appropriate for the age and ability of the cyclists. For less able cyclists, choose an organized event with an easy route and no worries of traffic.
- Train for the event; this doesn't have to be arduous, but fun family cycle rides can increase in distance over a period of time.
- Insist that youngsters wear helmets and always wear yours, to lead by example.
- Stick together; encourage each other when anyone gets tired or demotivated.
- Keep hydrated – drink plenty of water.

ELLA'S JOKE

Why did the little boy take his bicycle to bed with him?

—

Because he didn't want to walk in his sleep.

AMY SAYS...

When doing a really long cycle ride, you should pace yourself. You don't want to be too exhausted when you go over the finish line.

If you're doing a charity cycle ride, make it fun by dressing up to make yourself and the family stand out from the crowd. Wear silly outfits, paint your faces and decorate the bikes (safely).

DID YOU KNOW?

The Tour de France, established in 1903, is one of the most famous races in the world. It is considered to be one of the biggest tests of endurance.

CLEAN UP A **LOCAL** PARK

Clear up litter and weeds to make your local park more desirable for others.

Small playgrounds or parks can be a hub of activity for children in your locality, but not if they are overgrown or run down. Rather than ignore the issue, grumble about it or wait for something to be done, do your bit! By encouraging the children to 'voluntarily' work together to clean up a local amenity you will help them to understand and appreciate hard work often done by others.

It helps if the children have a vested interest in the location, possibly a park they use or have used in the past, and are therefore aware of how it has changed and been neglected. If it is a large area, focus on a section that will benefit others; children should understand that they are attempting to help others – possibly younger children than themselves – and that by giving up their time, they are committing selflessly to a local cause.

Once you've decided on your local spot, the hard work can begin! Chances are the ground will be covered in an abundance of weeds, ankle- and leg-stinging thistles, nettles and bramble briars, as well as unsightly litter. Be prepared and take with you a collection of gardening tools (hoe, rake, trowel, fork and spade) and trash bags. Depending on the state of the park, you'll need to dedicate a lot of time to pulling up weeds, clearing areas and removing litter. Everyone will need to work as a team, taking on different roles and

swapping them when the work gets tiring (which it will). But the effort will be worth it.

Don't forget to take a 'before and after' photograph to illustrate the impact of all your hard work. Revisit the site a week or so later to see if children have been playing and having fun there.

TIPS AND CONSIDERATIONS

- Wear suitable footwear and clothing to protect against stings and scratches.
- Wear gloves.
- Do not pick up any litter by hand. Use a litter picker or garden tool instead.

AMY SAYS...

This activity is also a great chance for us kids to have some fun!

WORK CONTRACT Make your parents sign a contract about your work. It could be something like 'If we work for half an hour we get five minutes play on the park.' After all, builders get a tea break – so why can't you have a play break?

DID YOU KNOW?

The slide was invented by Charles Wicksteed and was first put in a park in 1922.

ELLA'S JOKE

Why did the chicken cross the park?

—

To get to the other slide!

CLIMB INDOORS

Find an indoor climbing centre to see whether you have a head for heights.

You can never be too young or too old to try indoor climbing. If climbing to heights that make you feel woozy and light-headed (as if you are going to expire), are not your thing, then having a go at a climbing wall will push you out of your comfort zone – which can't be a bad thing, can it?

Most youngsters won't think twice about putting on a safety harness and scrabbling up a wall, placing their trust in three things: a harness (around their waist or body), a rope (fixed to their harness), and a belayer (the person attached to the other end of the rope, stood on the ground below the climber). Some children and adults, however, may need a little gentle coaxing, and if this is the case, they should not be rushed. Let worried climbers take their time to build up confidence in themselves and in the whole experience. A bad initial experience might put them off climbing for good, so encouragement and support are the watchwords.

Many climbing centres offer taster days, party packages and formal courses, as well as membership and equipment hire; they really do cater for all ages and abilities. Using a recognized provider gives you peace of mind that the equipment and walls are regularly inspected and maintained and are therefore safe and reliable. They are also accustomed to first-time or timid climbers and have ways of encouraging most people on to the wall.

Bouldering is another consideration for wannabe climbers or those families looking for indoor exercise and challenge. It doesn't involve ropes, so the aim is not to go as high as you can, but to complete graded routes, emphasizing technique and efficiency. Incidentally, bouldering is popular within the climbing community and competitions are regularly held for competitive types.

Look up your local climbing centre for information on how to get started or to find out when the next bouldering competition is being held.

ELLA'S JOKE

What goes up but never comes down?
—
Your age!

AMY SAYS...

Games to play at a climbing centre:

SHARK ATTACK Choose one person to be a 'shark'. All the others walk around in a swimming motion until the shark calls out 'Shark Attack'. Everyone then has to jump onto the climbing wall and grip the holds. If someone is caught, they're 'out'. No one can be caught if the WHOLE of their body is off the ground. Play until only one person remains.

LOOK NO HANDS See how high you can get without holding on (don't try this when bouldering or you could get seriously hurt!).

COMMUNITY WORK

Do your bit for the community – without being asked.

Being virtuous towards others has arguably become rarer, and perhaps even lost completely, in the increasingly cut-throat, fast-paced and self-centred life that makes up much of modern living. The term 'community' doesn't have the same meaning as it used to. Today, its emphasis leans towards 'place', with less focus than before on 'people'.

Reinstate the concept of true community and the idea that a virtuous act is a good thing. Make some time, every day, to complete a selfless act of kindness towards another person or animal. For young children, this could start close to home in the immediate vicinity of home, on something very small in scale. Then as children get older, the radius of virtue and scale of effort can be extended – but still within the local community.

On a grander scale, virtuous acts may entail joining a collective effort to raise money for a charity or a national/global cause.

Whatever the act of selflessness, it is the family dimension, or more specifically adult involvement, that is key here. It ensures that children are supervised and guided, and is also leading by example. Eventually the youngsters themselves will come to instigate their own community action and will perform virtuous tasks themselves.

Some simple ideas for virtuous activities close to home:

IN AND AROUND YOUR STREET
- Check on an elderly neighbour. Just by spending five minutes having a chat you could make someone's day, especially if they are lonely or unwell.
- Pick up litter on the streets around your home. Strangely, keeping streets free of litter is actually a deterrent to those who might be tempted to discard their rubbish.
- Make signs to encourage dog owners to be responsible and pick up after their dog(s).
- Offer to tidy up an elderly person's garden by weeding it for them.

IN THE WIDER COMMUNITY
- Organize a litter pick in your town or village centre.
- Open doors and let others through before yourself when out and about in shops etc.

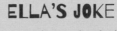

ELLA'S JOKE

David Beckham is at home when he hears a knock at the door. He answers it and meets the binman. The binman says,
'Alright Becks, where's yer bin?'
'I've been out the back with the kids,'
replies Beckham.
'No!' says the binman. 'Where's yer wheelie bin?'
'Alright! You got me. I've been on the loo!'

TIPS AND CONSIDERATIONS

- Use litter pickers.
- Children should wear gloves and be made aware of safety around sharp and undesirable objects.

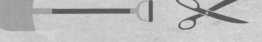

DID YOU KNOW?

The world's largest rubbish dump is larger than the USA and is found floating in the middle of the Pacific Ocean.

AMY SAYS...

Litter picking is a difficult and smelly task, but who cares? You can turn it into your own fun game by challenging each other to a competition to see who can collect the most litter in a set amount of time. Have different winning categories like 'laziest litter picker' or 'best bottle collector'. Make it completely your own and before you know it, it will be time to go home after your hard day's work.

DISCOVER LOCAL HISTORY

Find out about some interesting and 'horrible' history that is specific to the area.

History is on everyone's doorstep, and people often know less about their immediate locality than they do about places further afield. Help connect your children with the area in which you live by taking them out on investigatory walks, and encouraging them to be history detectives, on the search for clues about the past.

ELLA'S JOKE

Why were the early days of history called the dark ages?

—

Because there were so many knights.

TIPS AND CONSIDERATIONS

To motivate the kids into action, suggest a theme that will capture their interests and stimulate their imagination.
Here are some ideas:

- **DEATHS** Have there been any interesting or suspicious deaths in your locality, either recently or in the past? Find the gravestone of the oldest person to have died in the area.
- **GHOSTS** Is there any evidence of ghosts or supernatural occurrences in the area to explore?
- **DISEASE** In previous historical eras, have there ever been any cases of disease or infection – such as the Plague or leprosy?
- **HISTORICAL BUILDINGS** Are there any historically significant buildings or dwellings remaining in your local area?
- **ANCIENT CELEBRITIES** Did anyone well-known or famous live in your locality? Find out as much as you can about them and visit the places they lived or frequented.
- **MYTHS AND LEGENDS** Kids love stories, so mythical figures and beings naturally capture their imaginations. See if any myths and legends originate from your local area.

This adventure is perhaps best started at home with some old-fashioned research on the internet to whet the appetite before mobilizing the young history detectives into action.

If you are looking for ideas of things to do that require less effort, then look for prepared historical adventure trails and treasure hunts. This also applies to areas within your wider locality – such as a local wood, hill fort, monument or remains.

History is all around us; you just have to go and find it.

AMY SAYS...

Make a treasure hunt for others to follow. Give players some clues that lead them to different historical places and eventually a hidden treasure.

Act out a scene that could have happened in history. It could be a battle (NO ACTUAL FIGHTING THOUGH) or the coronation of a king/queen.

DID YOU KNOW?

The Great Pyramid of Giza in Egypt is the only wonder of the ancient world that is still standing.

EXPLORE YOUR LOCAL AREA
USING PUBLIC TRANSPORT

Find new ways to get around and see parts of your locality you haven't seen before.

Your local area is somewhere you are familiar with. You may walk and drive through it on a daily basis, but familiarity leads to complacency, so why not become more adventurous and truly explore what is around you? Use a local bus stop as your starting point. Purchase a day pass or group ticket from the bus driver and settle down for the first stage of your journey, leaving your local vicinity. The distance that you cover and areas that you visit will depend greatly on the town or city that you live in. The travel pass may include buses, trams, trains or bicycles to add variety to your use of public transport.

There are no set rules. You merely have to get off at different bus stops and get on different buses (or other forms of public transport),

it couldn't be simpler. The very nature of bus routes is that they visit different areas and take random routes in order to pick up passengers. By taking different routes you will be taken around parts of the city or town that you may have never seen before. Certain locations may have famous ties or links with celebrities and you may like to visit these areas to gain an insight into events or people.

DID YOU KNOW?

Horse-drawn buses were used in the early 1800s.

TIPS AND CONSIDERATIONS

- Before setting off, check a map of the local bus routes to get an idea of which areas are accessible.
- Make a note of where routes end and be careful not to venture too far out of the zones that you have paid for.
- Be prepared to walk between different stops.
- Be flexible with your schedule – if something takes your interest, then spend time exploring it further.

ELLA'S JOKE

Which famous explorer travelled using public transport?
—
Christopher Colum-bus!

How do trains hear?
—
Through their engine-ears!

AMY SAYS...

Exploring your local area gives you a great opportunity for people watching (or spying!). When you're sitting on buses, look around at the other passengers. Try to imagine what their names are and where they've come from and where they're going to. Be creative (or silly!).

When you're out and about, look out for unusual shop names. Businesses often use clever or silly names to make people laugh. Who can spot the silliest or cleverest?

FUN RUN FOR CHARITY

Whatever the distance, go on a run and raise some money for a good cause.

What could be better than the feeling of running and feeling fit? Well, there is something better; running, feeling fit AND feeling good!

The feel-good factor comes from running for a cause or a charity, so even if you are not a running family, a charity fun run is a must and the chances are, if you complete one, you won't stop there. They really are that enjoyable and rewarding.

Fun-run events offer a variety of distances (1m/1.7km, 3m/5km, 5m/8km) so there should be no excuses to do with age, fitness or ability.

Of course if people think they are going to have fun then they are more inclined to take part in the first place. Reluctant runners might need a little persuasion, so think creatively of ways to add appeal. Dressing up is often what appeals to children and this certainly adds to a sense of occasion. Fun runs for charity are particularly light-hearted and runners who are not in fancy dress actually tend to look out of place. So that means even the adults need to dress up and get into the spirit.

Once you have come to terms with dressing up, think of a theme for the family group. If you have a dog, and dogs are allowed to take part, include it in the equation too. This adds an extra fun dimension to the dressing-up

theme, and the dog also gets a an additional round of exercise – bonus!

Our favourite family theme is *Scooby Doo* and we even carry an MP3 player and speaker with us that plays the TV theme tune as we run.

TIPS AND CONSIDERATIONS

- Look for a charity event and try and run with other people – the collective power of persuasion works a treat.
- Pencil a date into the calendar early as this gives you a little time to prepare (notice we didn't say 'train').
- On the day, have a light breakfast and make sure runners are wearing socks and trainers (to prevent blisters).

AMY SAYS...

Although races are great fun, you need to make sure that you don't run really fast at the start, then tire yourself out so much that you end up dragging your feet over the finish line. So make sure that you start slowly and run at a steady pace; you can always sprint at the end if you have energy left!

A MEDAL AND A GOODY BAG

At most charity races they give you a goody bag and a medal when you cross the line. As well as having a huge amount of fun and raising money for charity, you get a prize too!

DID YOU KNOW?

Britain Roger Bannister was the first person to run a mile in under four minutes.

ELLA'S JOKE

Who is the fastest runner of all time?

—

Adam, because he came first in the human race!

GOING WITHOUT ELECTRICITY
LIGHTING

Twenty four hours without flicking a switch.

Going without electricity might not seem like a challenge, but it is surprisingly difficult and makes you realize how much we take electrical devices for granted. The idea is to not turn on anything electrical for 24 hours – that's from the moment you wake up until the moment you go to bed!

Modern western life relies upon electricity and as people become accustomed to using electrical devices in their everyday lives, they become reliant and dependent upon such items; particularly lighting. A power cut or short period without electricity provides a short shock, but choosing to do without

electricity for a whole day makes us question how much we need and use.

So for one day try to avoid turning on any lights, from the moment your eyes open. That means no light when brushing your teeth or when eating your breakfast.

As night falls, the house will take on a completely different atmosphere when candles and torches become the main light source. Add a splash of colour with glow sticks; these will last all night and provide a colourful glow to the room.

EQUIPMENT NEEDED

- Candles and matches.
- Torches.
- Glow sticks.

KEEPING SAFE

- Never leave candles unattended.
- Supervise young children near flames.
- Show children how to safely extinguish a candle.

AMY SAYS...

GAME TO PLAY

KEEPER OF THE KEYS This game is really simple to play. All you need is a chair, a set of keys and a scarf, or anything that can be used as a blindfold (not that you'll need one if you're playing it in the dark!). One person has to sit on the chair with the keys underneath. A person is picked to go and carefully get the keys from under the chair and get back to their place before the person on the chair ('the keeper of the keys') hears them and points at them. If the stealer does get caught (pointed at), then the keys are returned and someone else has a go.

DID YOU KNOW?

- Some glow sticks can last for more than 10 hours!
- Candles were the only forms of light in olden times, as well as fires.
- An average child, aged five to ten years old, needs 10-11 hours sleep!

ELLA'S JOKE

Why did the gardener plant a light bulb in his garden?

—

Because he wanted to grow a power plant.

GOING WITHOUT ELECTRICITY
COOKING

Modern kitchens are full of electrical gadgets that we rely on every single day; microwaves, cookers and even toasters are the devices that we use to heat up our breakfast, lunch and dinner. Without electricity, none of these will work... and that's where the adventure begins!

Challenge yourselves to go without electricity for 24 hours but still cook family meals in the home – takeaways would be cheating so therefore are not allowed! One solution would be to simply eat cold food and picnic throughout the day. This wouldn't be part of an adventure though, since it is too easy an option, so why not bring the camping solution indoors and cook meals on a gas camping stove? Plan a simple one-pot meal that can be cooked quickly on the stove and then enjoyed together. Remember not to put the dirty plates in the dishwasher at the end!

One alternative might be a barbeque for one or all of the meals – take your cooking outside, even in the colder weather. Heat up your choice of meat and vegetables and then eat alfresco or indoors by candlelight.

Going without electricity for 24 hours helps to encourage a long-term awareness of this energy source. Consider fitting an electricity monitor to inform you which appliances in the house use the most electricity. A greater awareness might lead to a positive impact on your utility bills!

TIPS AND CONSIDERATIONS
- Plan your meals before the day – keep it simple, make it fun and memorable!
- Get the kids involved with the food preparation and cooking.

EQUIPMENT NEEDED
- Gas stove/barbecue.
- Matches or fire lighter.

AMY SAYS...

THE 'I'M (NOT) A CELEBRITY, GET ME OUT OF HERE' CHALLENGE

Test your taste buds with a 'mystery foods challenge' in the dark. Find some tasty and yucky foods and get a family member to taste them — can they guess what they are?

Instead of tasting foods that differ, you could choose the same food or drink but try different brands — can you work out which is which?

ELLA'S JOKE

Why is wind power so popular?
—
Because it has lots of fans.

DID YOU KNOW?

Solar ovens use the power of the sun to cook food and can even work on overcast days.

GOING WITHOUT ELECTRICITY
ENTERTAINMENT

The digital world that we live in provides us with seemingly endless entertainment. Many people often choose the television or a computer as a quick and easy form of passing the time. But what would happen if there were a power cut or, due to weather storms, the power were off for a few days? These events could happen at any time and certainly make us aware of how much we count on our electrical supply.

For this adventure, you are challenged to not turn on anything electrical – so no computer games, no internet, no television! It's back to basics and hopefully back to some good quality family time.

During daylight hours, life is much easier and everyone can get on with their activities. As darkness falls and visibility becomes more difficult, some adjustments may need to be made (see Lighting, page 84). Use the darkness to play a range of family games, both indoors and outdoors:

NIGHTLINE

Attach a piece of string to a door handle (this will be the starting point) and then thread it round the room – under tables, behind the sofa and over chairs. Everybody begins at the starting point and follows each other around the room, giving advice, instructions and support to one other. This game could also be played outside.

ZAP TAG

One person holds a torch and is 'it'. The torch is not turned on. When the person with the torch sees another person he/she turns the torch on and must shine it on the other person to zap him/her. If you want to be very strict about not using electricity, then you can use a wind-up torch.

TIPS AND CONSIDERATIONS

- Keep a selection of board games that are age-appropriate for all members of the family. Popular board games take on a different feel when played by candlelight.
- Keep active – don't just sit around – choose games that require people to get up and move around.
- Have a range of games prepared so that no-one gets bored; children can easily become distracted and disengaged, therefore be prepared to swap the activities as and when needed.

ELLA'S JOKE

What would a bare-footed
man get if he stepped on
an electrical wire?
—
A *pair of shocks!*

DID YOU KNOW?

Electric currents are measured
in amperes (amps).

AMY SAYS...

When it gets dark, it's fun to play hide and seek or sardines
in the house or garden:

Get everyone to wait outside. The first person goes into the
house or garden and finds somewhere to hide, while everyone
else counts to 60. Everyone else (the seekers) then go their
separate ways, trying to find the hider. If someone finds the
hider they mustn't shout out, but hide with them (become
a sardine). The last person to find everyone is the new hider.

Another bit of fun you can have is to play Twister in
the dark. You'll need to wear headtorches so you can see
the coloured spots. Be careful not to shine the light in
anyone's eyes!

HAVE A GREEN DAY

Do all you can for the environment in one day.

This is more of a challenge than an adventure perhaps, but sometimes making a simple change to our everyday habits and lifestyle choices tests our powers of resilience and determination as much as any physical challenge may do.

Environmental issues such as global warming, rising sea levels and green energy regularly appear in the news. Nowadays people are becoming more aware of the issues, but little is done to combat them.

World Environment Day has been celebrated on 5 June every year since 1973. It aims to raise awareness of environmental issues that are affecting the planet. Earth Day is another annual event that is celebrated on 22 April. People all over the world celebrate and hold events to promote respect for the Earth's environment.

So, you could hold your own 'Green Day' in which you promote green issues at your own local level.

ACTIVITIES TO DO ON YOUR GREEN DAY:

- Plant trees – simply plant a tree in your garden or school or offer to help planting trees at an organized event.
- Pick up litter in the local area.
- Switch off lights and electrical appliances that aren't being used.
- Recycle and reuse materials – promote this by creating posters for your local area.
- Only buy and eat locally grown produce.
- Don't use the car or any vehicle for the day; Instead, walk, scooter or cycle everywhere.

TIPS AND CONSIDERATIONS

- Choose a theme for your 'Green Day'; focus on one key issue, such as water. Millions of people die each year from water shortages, lack of sanitisation and hygiene-related illnesses; these deaths happen mainly in developing countries. We take water for granted and use it without thinking. 'During your Green Day', make a concerted effort to become aware of how much water you use.
- Turn off the taps when brushing your teeth.
- Collect rainwater in an outdoor butt.
- Have a shower, not a bath. If you have a shower, try to see how quick you can be (under four minutes). Are you brave and adventurous enough to have a shower outside, from a water butt?
- Use a plug in the sink when washing your face or shaving.
- Use a bowl for washing food and vegetables, then use the same water to rinse out cans, jars and bottles for recycling.
- Only use the dishwasher when it's full.
- Place a Save-a-flush bag in your toilet cistern to reduce the amount of water used for flushing.

AMY SAYS...

Recycling is important; it uses less money and energy but more importantly saves more of the earth's resources. So do your bit by first of all reducing the amount of waste you produce (i.e. buy things with less packaging); re-using materials (e.g. plastic bags, water bottles etc.) and recycling (paper, glass, tins etc.).

You might know all this already, but why don't you help others become more aware of the issue? Create posters or leaflets to put around your local area. If you're brave enough, write an article that could be printed in your school newsletter or local newspaper.

DID YOU KNOW?

97% of the water on Earth is saltwater and only 3% is freshwater. Approximately 2% is frozen in glaciers and ice caps.

ELLA'S JOKE

Global warming is an anagram of 'ball going warm'.

MAKE A **STAND** AND **SUPPOR**T A **CAUSE**

Do your bit and make a point about something you believe in.

Sometimes there is an issue that grabs the attention or appeals to the heart, whether local, national or international. Adults and children alike can be hooked enough to express an opinion or to raise attention to the cause.

There might be something happening locally that triggers a reaction, such as the building of unwanted houses or services; or the removal/destruction of a much-loved venue (e.g. a footpath, a library or a swimming pool). Your child(ren) might watch something on television or be studying an issue at school that leads to further investigation at home.

Showing support for an issue encourages children to express opinions, debate topics and appreciate different points of view. Spend time discussing the issue and the reasons for and against the decisions around it, then develop their personal reaction by asking questions that stimulate further thinking.

So how do you make a stand and support a cause? Find out if a local group is holding a protest about the issue; you can then support them and the cause by attending. Numbers are important, so the more people that are there showing allegiance, the better.

MAKING A STAND ABOUT DOG MESS IN YOUR LOCAL AREA

- **SURVEY THE SITUATION** Make sure there's a problem to protest about first.
- **GENERATE AWARENESS** Make posters and display them to draw attention to the issue.
- **OFFER A SOLUTION** Provide dog poo bags for people to use – this gives no excuses.
- **TELL THE MEDIA** A local newspaper or TV channel might help spread the word.

AMY SAYS...

The high tide line on a beach is often littered with a mixture of non-biodegradable plastic rubbish brought in by the sea. Why not raise awareness by collecting it up and turning it into a sea monster. Place your finished monster on the beach for passers-by to see. Don't forget to recycle it at the end of the day.

ELLA'S JOKE

Why don't dogs make good dancers?
—
Because they've got two left feet!

DID YOU KNOW?

Read about 10 year-old Vivienne Harr from www.makeastand.com who, when she was only eight years old, wanted to make a BIG stand; she wanted to end child slavery. She has raised lots of money, appeared on TV and in newspapers with her campaigning. Take some inspiration from Vivienne and change the world.

'You don't have to be big or powerful to change the world. You can be just like me.'
Vivienne Harr

MOTHER'S DAY ONE-POT

Treat mum to a tasty one-pot lunch in the fresh air, away from the crowds.

Mother's Day is a special occasion, so be sure you make it one to remember! This particular activity is bound to create good memories as it's always the thought and effort that count on this annual celebration.

Interested? First let's define what a one-pot lunch is. The idea is simple. It's a warm healthy lunch cooked on a stove, using only one pot (pan). The fact that you need very little in the way of pans, crockery and cutlery means you'll be able to carry everything you need in a medium-sized rucksack (or tuck-sack as we like to call it).

There's no need to feel restricted to cooking on a stove – you may not have one. Instead build a fire or use a disposable BBQ.

For meal ideas there are many options and anything goes, so you'll be able to create a variation of most meals in just one pot.

HERE ARE SOME OF OUR FAVOURITE ONE-POT RECIPES:

- **TUNA AND PASTA BAKE** Pasta shapes cooked in a tomato sauce with tuna and your favourite vegetable (e.g. peas, sweetcorn, pepper).
- **SPAGHETTI CARBONARA** This simple version combines spaghetti with chopped-up ham in a crème fraîche and grated cheese sauce.
- **SWEET AND SOUR CHICKEN** Use pre-cooked chicken for ease and speed. Add the meat to noodles in a tomato, vinegar and soy sauce mixture along with mange tout, baby corn and chopped pineapple chunks.
- **SALMON COUSCOUS** Boil the couscous with the salmon (chopped) and vegetables (e.g. carrots, beans, pepper) in stock. Add a tomato sauce for a really Mediterranean feel.

LOCATIONS TO CONSIDER

- **FOREST** Eat with the birds and the squirrels.
- **BEACH** Enjoy a meal on your own favourite secluded beach.
- **MOUNTAIN** Feel like you are eating on top of the world.
- **RIVER** Listen to the soothing sounds of a river or the liveliness of a babbling brook.

TIPS AND CONSIDERATIONS

Boil the base of the meal (rice, pasta, lentils etc.) in the pan first, adding vegetables part-way through. Remove them from the pan when tender so you can cook the meat or sauce. Next, re-add the base ingredients to the sauce and reheat. It is as simple as that.

AMY SAYS...

Make the day even more special for your mum by taking along flowers or bulbs that you have grown yourself. NB This involves forward planning!

Play a Mother's Day version of 'I went to the shop and bought a....' such as 'While cooking, I ...' or to be more adventurous, 'While out in the jungle hunting wild buffalo, I...'

DID YOU KNOW?

The celebration of Mother's Day as we know it today, began in the United States in the early 20th century. Mothering Sunday is an older event that celebrated the Mother Church.
The two are not related.

ELLA'S JOKE

Two mums having a chat:
Mum 1: How do you manage to get your lazy-head kid up in the mornings?
Mum 2: I put the cat on the bed.
Mum 1: How does that help?
Mum 2: The dog's already there!

SCOOTER SAFARI

Explore your local area – by micro-scooter!

Despite what you are thinking, scooters are not just for children; in fact they offer lots of potential for self-powered adventure, suitable for adults and youngsters alike.

The main consideration before setting off to scooter is the terrain. Scooters are only really effective on smooth, stone-free surfaces. This makes them ideal for cycle paths, riverside and canal-side towpaths, as well as pedestrian areas and footpaths. Some degree of planning, or at least forethought, is required to ensure smooth running.

The magic of this adventure is experienced when you witness the change of landscape and features during a safari from a rural area into the centre of a city. Fields and farmland full of grazing (and often curious) animals punctuated by the added interest of an

occasional weir or lock. Houseboats lining rivers or canals banks become an indicator of human inhabitance and activity as you travel along.

When the safari gets closer to the city or town, the amount of concrete that features in the environment gradually increases. Footpaths, bridges and overpasses all become ever more common and as the city centre looms nearer, modernity is partly replaced by historical waterways and transportation links of old.

Once you have navigated the city or town centre waterways and reached your agreed destination, either head back along the same route (if your route is not circular), or catch a bus back to your start point. A bus journey will need forward planning.

TIPS AND CONSIDERATIONS

- Make sure young scooter riders always wear a helmet.
- Take plenty of snacks and water to keep riders fuelled up and hydrated.
- Plan a safari with some awareness of how much time you will need – particularly if you are intending to catch a bus home.

AMY SAYS...

GO TO FAMOUS PLACES AROUND THE CITY

If you manage to get into the city, try to visit a well-known place such as a sportsground or a landmark. Find out something about it you didn't know already such as when it was built and why.

COUNT THE CARS

This is a great game for exhausted riders. Find a bench somewhere in town, sit down and start counting car colours. Each player chooses a coloured car and then counts how many of that colour they can see. The one who sees the most of that colour wins. Once you're powered up from a rest and have finished the game, set off again on your journey.

DID YOU KNOW?

Scooters have been around for over a century and were first made by attaching roller-skate wheels to a wooden board with handles made of cardboard boxes!

ELLA'S JOKE

What do you call a thieving alligator?
—
A crookodile!

WAKE AND RUN

Go for an early morning run – it's the best way to start the day.

It takes a lot of effort to get up early and go for a run, especially on a weekend at the end of a busy week, but once you've completed it, you're guaranteed to feel happier, healthier and certainly more awake.

This activity is simply about getting up, getting out and doing it. You don't need expensive trainers or running kit. Anyone, anywhere can get up earlier than normal and go for a gentle jog or exertive workout.

If you do head out early with your children, you'll all see your locality in a slightly different way – and this is what gives this simple, everyday activity an adventurous feel. Whether it's seeing the milkman on his early morning rounds, watching an urban fox heading home after a night of scavenging, or hearing the early dawn chorus heralding the start of a new day, you will feel differently about the world, in a very positive way.

Local running clubs or national organizations that are aiming to increase levels of exercise and participation in sport often run initiatives in local parks and public spaces, so look on the internet for your nearest opportunity.

Running is a very social activity, so invite some friends and neighbours on a run with you early one morning. They may initially think you are a bit bonkers, but encourage them to give it a go and they are bound to appreciate the benefits. You may even find yourself starting your own local family running club.

AMY SAYS...
WINTER WONDERLAND

Head out early on a frosty morning and leave fresh footsteps in snow or frost. You could try and make patterns with the footprints your feet create, or walk in an unusual way to create fun shapes.

Write the messages in the dew or in the frost on benches and picnic tables for others to read later in the day — maybe you could write motivational comments if there are joggers around or if there is a charity run later on during the day.

Observe the magical ice crystal formations of fence posts and gates — if it has been frosty the night before, you may see quite a lot of frost scattered around.

Skate on frozen puddles and watch the ice crack and fragment beneath your feet — do make sure it isn't a deep puddle or you may get very cold feet if the water flows over the rim of your shoes.

ELLA'S JOKE

What steps do you take if you
see a tiger running towards you?
—
Big ones!

DID YOU KNOW?

The most consecutive marathons run in
a single year is 365 and was completed
by Belgian runner Stefaan Engels, who
was aged 49 when he finished!

HILLS AND
MOUNTAINS

HILLS AND MOUNTAINS

Nothing is more exhilarating than standing at the summit of a hill or mountain, appreciating the wonderful view and feeling on top of the world.

How about sleeping on a mountain, attempting three peaks in three days or finding a waterfall and walking behind it? Climbing a mini 'Matterhorn' or undertaking a winter summit walk are other exciting options for exploring the higher reaches of our natural surroundings.

CLIMB A MINI MATTERHORN

Walk and climb a matterhorn-shaped hill near you.

This adventure is based on climbing a large hill or mountain that bears some resemblance to one of the world's most dramatic looking and dangerous summits, the Matterhorn in the Swiss Alps. You can't fail to enjoy the exhilaration and excitement that follows an energetic climb up to a conical summit.

There are many Matterhorn-like peaks, so find one that is fairly local to where you live and pick a day on which the weather will allow stunning views. That way, all your physical exertion will be so much more satisfying and worthwhile.

Take in the fantastic 360° panoramic views; then stake a claim that you have climbed a mini Matterhorn.

Talk to your children about the Swiss Matterhorn beforehand, and even show them some photos or videos to help them relate to the mini Matterhorn they are about to walk up. Talk up the whole thing as much as you can and your children will think they are climbing something bigger and more exciting than they actually are. Tag on a few extra miles before or after the climb and the result will be that, to little legs, it will feel like a full-on expedition.

Take a bag for litter and a litter-picker so you can encourage your children to hunt for trash as they walk; this not only takes their minds off the miles, but means the mini Matterhorn will become a cleaner place.

SUGGESTED MINI MATTERHORNS FOR YOU TO CLIMB

- **Shutlingsloe**
  Peak District
- **Belles Knot**
  Lake District
- **Roseberry Topping**,
  North Yorkshire Moors
- **Suilven**
  North West Highlands

TIPS AND CONSIDERATIONS

- Be prepared for a change in weather, particularly if the Matterhorn you are climbing is of a fair size.
- Walking poles or sticks will help with any steep descents.
- As ever, with any exertion, take snacks and drinks with you.

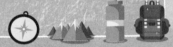

ELLA'S JOKE

Why are mountain climbers curious?
—
They always want to take another peak.

DID YOU KNOW?

The Swiss Matterhorn is:
1 4478m (or 14,692ft) high.
2 One of the most famous mountains
   in the world.
3 One of the highest mountains
   in the Alps.

AMY SAYS...

Here is an idea to help time pass:
THE SPELLING GAME Somebody
says a letter. Then another person adds
a letter, beginning to spell out a word.
Continue to add letters until you come
to an end of a word. The person who
adds the final letter looses.

HINT – *you can add the letter 's' to
the end of many words.*

CLIMB A WINTER SUMMIT

Climb a hill or mountain in snowy conditions – fun, but a bit scary.

Climbing a summit towards the end of the winter offers a great experience for a young hill walker. Cold air, bright skies and crispy ice drifts below your feet all combine to make a fulfilling and memorable adventure.

Treat this undertaking with the respect it deserves though. The snowy or icy conditions and sub-zero temperatures make the hills and mountains potentially dangerous places to be with youngsters. Plan meticulously, take the appropriate equipment, and climb with someone who is experienced and competent if you feel at all out of your depth. In fact, if you have any doubts at all about a proposed trip, don't go on this occasion; wait until it feels right.

TIPS AND CONSIDERATIONS

- Even if the weather looks like it will be kind to you, make sure that you are well prepared for a sudden deterioration or for general temperature changes.
- Take extra clothing layers to put on when they are needed.
- Like most walking adventures, make sure you tell someone where you are going and when you expect to be back.
- Food and fluids are essential, as are a map and compass.
- It's worth taking a walking stick or pole of some kind – especially valuable when descending slippery sections.
- If the going gets too tough or dangerous, do the right thing and turn back – it's a braver decision than to carry on when your instinct says call it a day!

AMY SAYS...

BODY SLEDGING Find a relatively flat, safe slope to slide down on your back. It's great fun, but make sure you have an adult check that there is a safe stopping zone and that there are no unexpected dangers. Be careful – while a sledge has a brake, you don't, so be careful not to go out of control!

Search the downwind edges of walls and fences for snowdrifts. It's fun to step gingerly along the tops of drifts, but be ready for a sudden fall into the deep snow beneath you!

DID YOU KNOW?

The highest summit on Earth is Mount Everest, 8848m (29,000ft) above sea level. At the summit temperatures range between -20°C to -35°C with wind speeds of up to 280kmph (174mph).

ELLA'S JOKE

What did one mountain say to the other?

—

Let's meet in the valley!

CLIMB AND ABSEIL

Climb a rock and abseil down – with ropes of course.

Climbing outdoors is a natural next step to make after mastering the physical and psychological challenge of indoor climbing. Outside, the potential for plenty of fresh air, sunshine and great views makes this a very enjoyable family adventure. Take your dog and a picnic, and there is no better way to spend a summer's day!

CLIMBING INDEPENDENTLY

This is obviously more of a challenge, as you need your own equipment and you need to be confident and competent enough to set up some outdoor climbs safely. You are fully responsible for you and your climbers' safety. Part of this involves knowing where to climb i.e. finding routes that are within the grasp of your climbers, and within your ability to either safely lead-climb or setup a top/bottom rope system. And of course, you need to be a competent belayer and able to tie the required knots.

CLIMBING WITH SOMEONE EXPERIENCED

If you are climbing with someone experienced e.g. as part of a course laid on by an accredited climbing group, then much of the safety considerations and precautions will be managed by the instructor; they should have the skills and experience to run a safe outdoor climbing session. Also, it is likely that the equipment will be provided. If you are at all unsure of your climbing abilities or how to use the climbing equipment you have, then this is the route you need to take.

TIPS AND CONSIDERATIONS

- Always wear a helmet and insist others do too.
- Insist on regular 'buddy checks' between climber and belayer to ensure knots are tied correctly, harnesses are tight and carabineers are locked.
- Never let someone climb unless you are 100% confident in the system you have, and your ability to get a climber off the rock safely regardless of any event.
- If ever you have any doubts, stop, pack-up and try again another time – perhaps after some more tuition or training.
- Look after your equipment and check it regularly for wear and tear.

ELLA'S JOKE

Do you go rock climbing?
—
I would if I were boulder!

DID YOU KNOW?

A tall rock face called El Capitán in California is one of the world's favourite challenges for rock climbers.

AMY SAYS...

HELPFUL TIPS

1 FLAGGING Stick your foot out to the side to help you keep your balance.
2 LOOK DOWN occasionally to see where the next hold is — it doesn't make you a bad climber if you do.
3 SWAP FEET If you realize there's a hold on the other side of you that is in reach of your foot, swap feet.

FIND A WATERFALL

Locate, and walk to, an unusual waterfall to appreciate its form and grandeur.

Waterfalls vary in size, shape and form, but regardless of how powerful or dramatic a waterfall may be, you can guarantee a great view, somewhere that's exciting to explore and a super picnic spot – or all three!

The walk to a waterfall can vary too, depending on the surrounding geology and landscape. Different trails of varying lengths can guide you through magical woodland scenery or rocky gorges, revealing glimpses of lively cascades of water or dramatic drops into sculptured plunge pools. Sometimes a walk may be dotted with different waterfalls whereas others might lead up to a single, spectacular sight.

Finding a waterfall is easy since there are many trails in the countryside dedicated to discovering and appreciating this natural wonder. But there are places where waterfalls are hidden, and the challenge is to find them,

because they are off the beaten track. It can be rewarding to discover an unexpected waterfall without the need to follow a tourist track.

Waterfalls are very dramatic but you must be prepared to observe variations in flow due to changing weather conditions. Obviously the best time to visit a waterfall is after a period of heavy rainfall, when you'll be guaranteed a greater flow.

Waterfalls provide a spectacular and picturesque backdrop for any picnic but for the more daring, try a dip into the river or plunge pool at the bottom. It will be great fun, refreshing and possibly chilly!

TIPS AND CONSIDERATIONS

- Wear suitable footwear.
- Take waterproofs (and a swimming costume, change of clothes and a towel if you're planning on going for a dip).
- Appreciate nature from different angles on the walk – try to spot new and interesting plant life, and look at rock formations from a different viewpoint. You might even glimpse a rainbow in the right light!

DID YOU KNOW?

The highest steady-flowing waterfall, Angel Falls in Venezuela, got its name when American pilot Jimmie Angel's plane was damaged after landing on top of the falls. Angel and his three companions were forced to walk down the mountain, hence the falls are now called 'Angel' Falls!

AMY SAYS...

Chances are the waterfall has a boring name. See if you can give it a more exciting name. Tell the world the name by writing it with sticks, stones, pebbles and other bits and bobs.

ELLA'S JOKE

Where can you find a waterfall with no water?
—
On a map.

GO BEHIND A WATERFALL

Appreciate the view – and the noise – from the other side.

Walking to a waterfall, then pausing to watch it and listen to it while feeling its awesome power, is a thrilling experience in itself, for both adults and children. But imagine the breathtaking feeling of walking behind a waterfall!

Well don't just try and imagine the feeling, why not experience it for yourself?

Have a browse on the internet for potential waterfalls to visit – either locally, or further afield if you are on holiday or out on a day trip. But remember, you're not necessarily looking for spectacular waterfalls to visit. For this adventure, you need to identify a waterfall that has an overhang providing

clearance behind the falling water for you to walk behind.

Ideally, make your visit after a wet period, when you know there is going to be lots of water around. The larger volume of flowing water will make for a stunning natural spectacle.

Also, don't wait for a warm, dry day to complete this adventure. The fact that you get damp on the approach, then wetter still when behind the fall, makes this an activity of choice for a wet or miserable day.

TIPS AND CONSIDERATIONS

- Expect to get wet!
- Wear sturdy footwear as the approach may be rocky and slippery.
- Make sure excited youngsters don't get too far away from you – the noise of the water will make it difficult for you to communicate with them (should you need to).
- Expect to get wet!
- Take a picnic – waterfalls make for one of the nicest picnic locations.
- Expect to get wet!! (have we already said that)?

DID YOU KNOW?

Niagara Falls, on the border between Canada and USA, has the highest flow rate in the world.

ELLA'S JOKE

Why did the boy throw a glass of water out of the window?

—

He wanted to see a waterfall.

AMY SAYS...

Take some shampoo with you and give your hair a rinse (just like you see in the adverts). Make sure you use an environmentally friendly brand!

Feeling brave? Take a dip in the plunge pool. It will be very cold, so be warned. Also, make sure you get permission from an adult, and take one with you.

GO ON A NIGHT HIKE

Navigate and hike in the darkness.

A night hike is a popular activity within the wide range of children's groups affiliated to the Scouting movement. This is because a night hike, with a navigational element, offers a real sense of challenge and gives genuine satisfaction on completion.

The key to building up successful night hiking experiences is slowly, slowly:

WALK TOGETHER

Take your first night-time steps together as a family, perhaps in your local area. Walking at night will feel different and less familiar than during the daytime, so make sure young children feel safe and secure – you don't want to freak them out and put them off.

TAKE ON A NEW ROUTE

Again, keep it local, but this time plot a route that is new to you. Plan the hike on a map while still in the comfort of your own home. That way you won't know the details of what you are likely to encounter before you start walking. Set off after sunset and explore the new area by torch or moonlight.

INCREASE THE CHALLENGE A BIT

Head out beyond your locality for a short walk that you may have done before in the daytime. Choose a route that requires a map to follow it. Complete the same walk but this time in darkness, using a torch (or head torch) to read the map.

BEARING ON THE RIDICULOUS!

This challenge takes a bit of preparation, but it's worth it. Once again, take a short walk you are familiar with, but leave the kids at home so you can note down the compass bearings and directions of paths and junctions. The idea is to give the children enough information for them to be able to find their way in the dark (e.g. 'walk north for 10 minutes then at a junction, take the path on a bearing of 35 degrees. Follow that until you get to a stile etc.'). They may even do it unsupervised!

TIPS AND CONSIDERATIONS

- Start simply, then carefully build up the level of challenge – ensure children feel comfortable in the dark before you stretch them too much.
- A good head torch is a valuable investment and gives confidence to young walkers when they feel their path is well illuminated.
- At certain points in a night walk, turn the torches off and just stand, look and listen.
- Radio walkie-talkies are useful accessories for keeping walkers in touch with each other – and children with adults.

AMY SAYS...

Activities to do while hiking at night:

- Find a map that isn't special to your family, or needs keeping in pristine condition. As you're walking along, write down things you saw on the map and pinpoint them (Deer eyes in the dark, huge muddy puddles, junctions etc.).
- Keep track of where you're going — it may seem boring, but it is an important job to have — using a map might help!
- Play Imaginary Dot-to-Dot with the stars to see if they form any funny shapes!

ELLA'S JOKE

Did you hear about the Scout who sat up all night wondering where the Sun was?
—
It dawned on him the next morning!

DID YOU KNOW?

The compass was invented in China over 200 years before the birth of Christ.

NIGHT-TIME DESCENT

Descend a hill in the dark, after watching the sunset end and the stars appear.

Adventure can often be found in a place that is familiar during the day but looks and feels different at night, when conditions and ambience are often altered, especially on a hilltop or mountain. Set out for a peak during late afternoon or early dusk so that you can time yourself to reach the summit around nightfall.

Part of the fun of this activity comes from travelling against the flow of walkers heading down, towards their cars or homes for the night. The strange and questioning looks you will receive when heading 'upwards' will confirm that you are in fact doing something unusual (or adventurous).

During the ascent your eyes will get accustomed to the dimming light, and you are unlikely to need to use torchlight, especially if there is a moon of any kind.

Marvel at the soft glow of lamps and lights that mark the dwellings in villages and hamlets within the dark – and now featureless – landscape.

It is a very peaceful time and one to enjoy. Savour your walk in this serene and uncluttered moment. Listen carefully, think and ponder. Encourage youngsters to do this as well (modern living is increasingly pressurized, and opportunities for children to contemplate and reflect are rare).

TIPS AND CONSIDERATIONS

- Take a flask of soup and bread with you for a warming snack at the summit.
- Take along binoculars or a telescope to help with star and planet watching.
- Head torches are a good idea for the descent.
- If you parked in a car park, make sure you don't get locked in (car parks are often locked after the hours of darkness).
- If you take your dog, make sure they have a light on them. A dog may be a little disorientated by the darkness and could wander off.

AMY SAYS...

The summit of a hill at night is ideal for a spot of stargazing. Try to look for familiar constellations in the night sky, such as Orion or Cassiopeia (a W shape). If you can, learn and spot the constellation for your birth sign, for example Cancer is the constellation for July and is a crab shape.

On the way down, keep a look out for the reflections of your torchlight in eyes of night animals. Can you work out which nocturnal creature the eyes belong to?

DID YOU KNOW?

Eating carrots really can help your vision. Carrots contain vitamin A which helps us see!

ELLA'S JOKE

A boy and a knight were talking.
The boy said to the knight, 'How do you
see so well in the dark? Carrots?'

—

'No,' the knight replied. 'I was from the
dark ages. That's why I have Knight vision!'

PLAN AN EPIC SUMMIT

Pick a challenging mountain to 'bag'. The higher it is the better!

'Bagging a mountain' is a cool, adventurous saying that means a mountain has been climbed or conquered. Youngsters think it's awesome to be able to say they 'bagged' this mountain or that mountain, and it follows that the size of the 'bagged' summit is an extremely important factor. How many people, for example, can say that they have bagged Everest or the Eiger?

Planning to climb something on a more epic scale (epic as determined by the age and ability of the youngest adventurer) requires more preparation, training and experience. This needs to be taken seriously in order to ensure the challenge is safe, achievable and importantly, enjoyable.

Involving children in the planning and preparation phase helps them take on board the nature of the challenge, and it also gives them more ownership of it. Ownership intrinsically motivates a young walker to continue when things get tough and hard going (this is guaranteed if your summit is an epic one).

Climbing a proper summit is a good opportunity to teach young adventurers about 'layer management' . This is the process of putting on layers of clothes and taking them off as necessary in order to prevent excessive sweating and to stop you becoming vulnerable to drops in temperature or to wind chill.

TIPS AND CONSIDERATIONS

- Tell someone where you are going and when you expect to return.
- Check the local weather forecast – ideally provided by the local mountain rescue service.
- Carry clothing for different weather conditions – the weather on the top of a summit is likely to be very different to the weather on the ground.
- Take a map and compass, and know how to use them – don't rely on a mobile phone to work when out and about on a mountain.
- Take plenty of spare food and drinks, a first aid kit and even an emergency blanket if possible.

AMY SAYS...

SING SOME SONGS They are very motivational and take your mind off walking. How about 'When the Going gets Tough, the Tough get Going' (short but meaningful) or 'Ain't no Mountain High Enough' (a famous pop song that suits this occasion perfectly).

DID YOU KNOW?

In some places, weathering has worn away entire mountains! It takes many years for this process to work though, so it won't happen overnight.

ELLA'S JOKE

Why can't you play hide-and-seek with mountains?
—
Because they PEAK!

SCRAMBLE

Scramble up to the top of a steep hill. No ropes allowed.

If you want an activity that tests your head for heights and has a real element of danger, try scrambling with your family. Scrambling is neither rock climbing nor hill walking; it falls somewhere in between the two.

You know you are scrambling when you have to use both your hands and your feet in order to ascend or descend.

Scrambling is actually a climbing discipline in its own right, and can be done at all levels: from beginners, families and youngsters, to full-on hardcore graded scrambles. Some scrambling requires the use of climbing rope and possibly crampons (in winter) but families new to this activity should begin with short, easy scrambles.

TIPS AND CONSIDERATIONS

- Consider using an outdoor adventure provider or guide if you are new to scrambling. Such courses cover technique, equipment and safety, and build up your confidence in the process.
- Before you head out on your own, take a look on the internet for books on easy/beginner scrambling in your local area. A word of warning though; the weather and ground conditions will dictate how difficult or manageable a scramble is. An easy scramble after a period of wet weather for instance, will be much more challenging if slippery because of moisture and/or mud. Remember to use a guidebook as it is intended to be used; as a guide rather than an oracle of definitive advice.
- Occasionally stones or even loose rocks can become dislodged and fall. This can be very dangerous. Make sure your chosen location for a scramble is as free from loose material as possible, and encourage scramblers to climb with care.
- The wearing of helmets is a must whenever there is the slightest risk of falling debris.
- If debris falls, shout 'below' and drill all scramblers to look down, so that their helmets protect their heads.
- The sense of excitement and thrill felt only when there is a real sense of danger is guaranteed! So get outside and have a scramble – have fun, but keep safe.

DID YOU KNOW?

A difficult bit of scrambling is known as a 'bad step'.

AMY SAYS...

SCRAMBLE WORD GAME
Think of a word and spell it out, scrambling up the letters. The others have to try and guess what the word is by unscrambling the letters.

ELLA'S JOKE

How does a scrambler like his eggs?
—
Scrambled!

KIDS' TIPS (KIDS' VERSION!)
- If you're afraid of heights, don't look down, just in case.
- Pretend you're a mountain goat; keep all fours on something for security and try to keep balanced.
- At first, you might be a bit scared or worried, but just relax and you'll find it a lot easier than scrambling when scared.
- Don't be too confident — make sure you are still being safe and don't do anything too risky.

SKIING

Have a taste of this winter sport (not literally, of course).

Sometimes adventurous activities understandably cost money; whether that means equipment hire costs, specialist clothing needs or tuition (in the case of a new skill-based activity). Skiing is such a sport. It can end up being ridiculously expensive to go away to a 'celebrity' resort somewhere, but these days indoor ski slopes allow you to experience the thrill of skiing (on actual snow), for only a fraction of the cost of a skiing holiday.

Learn-to-ski packages are often relatively good value for money (shop around for deals). The quality of the coaching is usually very good and allows skiers to progress at their own pace; if someone is showing a natural ability, they should be fast-tracked and encouraged to ski independently.

A WORD OF CAUTION

If your children (and you) enjoy your time on the artificial snow, then you will be hankering to get into some real snow and onto some real mountains. For sure!

But if you are able to take a ski holiday during the off-peak season, and if you choose one of the budget resorts, like Pas de la Casa in Andorra or some of the other less glamorous options, you will be surprised how affordable skiing can be.

While we try and keep our adventuring costs to a minimum, we considered it a worthwhile expenditure to save up some money so that our girls could try 'real' skiing. It's so much fun!

AMY SAYS...

Here's some ski slope language to use when at the resort:

SNOW PLOUGH Turn the front ends of both your skis inward to form a V, but keep your legs shoulder-length apart. You use this movement to slow down.

PARALLEL TURNS Keep your skis parallel and lean into the slope when turning. Try to make your turn as small as possible.

WIPE OUT When someone knocks another skier over on the slope or when you crash or fall over.

ELLA'S JOKE

How many extreme skiers does it take to screw in a light bulb?

—

50: One to make the turns and then 49 to point up and say, 'I could have done that!'

DID YOU KNOW?

The word 'ski' comes from old Norse and actually means 'split piece of wood or firewood'.

SLEEP ON A MOUNTAIN

Spend a night in a bivvi bag on a hill or mountain and make the journey a challenge.

Imagine waking up in the morning with panoramic views of the surrounding countryside – what a great way to start the day. It doesn't begin there though; the adventure kicks off when you trek, with all your gear, up to your chosen location.

This adventure does not have to take place specifically on a hill or mountain, but should ideally be carried out at the highest point around. You can then enjoy not only the views, but also the feeling of being exposed to wind and weather conditions – a truly wild and exciting experience. Try to find a spot with a clear view from east to west so that you can see sunset and sunrise.

The distance you walk to your mountain-top sleeping spot will vary according to

the participants and should be considered and planned for accordingly. Another consideration will be the sleeping options; you could camp in tents, sleep under a tarpaulin, sleep in hammocks (if there are trees around) or sleep in bivvi bags. Whichever option you take, remember you'll have to carry all your equipment up to the chosen spot.

Sunrise will differ according to the time of year but why not get up at the crack of dawn and watch the sun creep up over the horizon to the sound of dawn birdcall?

TIPS AND CONSIDERATIONS

- Consider the age and ability of all those involved and choose a location that is appropriate.
- Check weather considerations and be prepared with appropriate clothing.
- Wear and take layers of clothing to allow for temperature changes throughout the day and night.
- Take water, a first aid kit and snacks with you to keep little ones (and big ones) happy.

AMY SAYS...

Games to play when on the way up or down a hill or in the tent/tarpaulin:

JUST KEEP ROLLING Be VERY careful in this game. Choose a hill with a slight slope and check the bottom is clear (no roads, fences or anything else dangerous). Then lie down and start to roll slowly down, making sure you don't go out of control. See where you end up — the exact place you thought you would? Make sure you have an adult's permission to play this game and have them close by, to stop you if you go too fast or in case anything dangerous happens.

20 QUESTIONS Someone thinks of an object or person. The other player then has to ask questions to try and find out what the person is thinking of. The main rule is that the person can only answer 'yes' or 'no' and the guesser has to ask, as the name suggests, 20, or less, questions.

ELLA'S JOKE

Where do fish sleep?
—
On a seabed!

DID YOU KNOW?

Within Great Britain and Ireland, a mountain is usually defined as any summit at least 610m (2000ft) high, while the official UK government's definition of a mountain is a peak of 600m (1958ft) or higher.

10 WAYS TO SLEEP OUTSIDE

Sleeping outside is an adventure that appeals equally as much to children as to adults. It's also one of the most exciting, yet easiest, outdoor activities. The excitement and thrill never wear off. And with a bit of practice, it's possible to have a night of sleep outdoors that is of better quality than any you might have in a bed indoors.

1 TENT

A tent is most people's preferred starting point for sleeping outdoors with the kids, even if it's only in your back garden, as it offers protection from the weather.

2 BIVVI BAG

A bivvi bag is like a waterproof jacket for your sleeping bag. You place it over your roll mat and sleeping bag to keep yourself protected from the wind and rain. The bonus is, you get to sleep with the breeze on your face, which is exhilarating.

3 TENSILE TREE TENT

A tree tent is suspended in the air and anchored on tree trunks, looking like a cross between a trampoline and a hammock under a waterproof flysheet. The result is an exciting and very comfortable shelter that is perfect for uneven terrain.

4 A HOMEMADE SHELTER

Whether you use a tarpaulin as the main structure or you are brave enough to build a shelter from scratch, you will need to build your own roof for the night. This is bound to make you sleep with a proud smile on your face.

5 HAMMOCK

One of the more romantic options perhaps, but equally practical. A pocket-sized shelter, it is ideal for lightweight travelling as it only requires two trees and two knots for fixing – and it keeps you off the ground, away from critters.

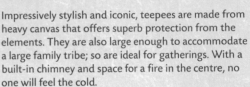

6 TEEPEE

Impressively stylish and iconic, teepees are made from heavy canvas that offers superb protection from the elements. They are also large enough to accommodate a large family tribe; so are ideal for gatherings. With a built-in chimney and space for a fire in the centre, no one will feel the cold.

7 ECOTENT

Ecotents are made from canvas or wood panelling. They are a simple, no-frills option for those who feel they require electricity (note we didn't say NEED). 'Tents' usually have electric lighting and a socket or two, but a lot of the other facilities for cooking and washing are shared, thus making them efficient and eco-friendly.

8 CAHUTTE

Cahuttes are a cross between a log cabin and a tent. They are double-floored with the ground floor being a plush log cabin with toilet and shower, kitchen and open-plan dining area. Upstairs, or should we say 'up ladder', the bedrooms are roofed and lined with canvas, so you actually feel as though you are camping.

9 BOTHY

A bothy is a basic shelter, often found in remote areas, usually on high ground. One good thing about a bothy is that it is traditionally free of charge. It will also allow you to go on extended ventures into the wild knowing you have a dry stop-off point along the way.

10 THE 'FAMILY BAG'

This is our own idea... or 'Ad-vention' (did you see what we did there?). The principle is to enable you to sleep outside together as a family, in a kind of DIY bivvi bag. Simply fold your tarpaulin in half and tie up the edges with some string. Then, drop in your roll mats and sleeping bags and snuggle down together inside your family bag. The joy of the family bag is in sharing the sleeping-out experience together in a fun and exciting way... and you can even include the family dog too.

THREE PEAKS IN THREE DAYS

As you may guess from the title, this adventure is one of the more challenging ideas put to you in this book. It requires a sustained effort over a period of days, the degree of which will be determined by what is realistically feasible for the youngest or least fit members of your family.

Peak choice, or more specifically peak definition, is important. A three-peak challenge for a family with young children might involve walking up three relatively small hills. Whereas a family with older and hardier walkers might take on three mountains – find out what the definition of a mountain is for your own particular region.

Another way to make the challenge more feasible is to choose peaks that you can drive between, so each day's walking is focused on the ascent and descents, rather than the walk between peaks.

The key thing is to sustain your effort over three consecutive days, because without wanting to sound sadistic, it's the cumulative fatigue in your legs and the depletion of energy reserves that makes this an endurance event; the kind of challenge that you don't enjoy as much during the experience as you do once it's completed.

TIPS AND CONSIDERATIONS

- Always be prepared for a change in weather, particularly when taking on higher peaks.
- Ensure walkers are wearing suitable footwear to avoid twisted ankles or bruised toes.
- Always carry a map of the area you are in.
- Take plenty of snacks and drinks to keep walkers fuelled up and hydrated.
- Have some ideas for games, songs and activities to do during the challenge – these take the mind off aches, pains and weary feelings.

DID YOU KNOW?

The UK National Three Peak challenge involves climbing Ben Nevis in Scotland, Scafell Pike in England and Snowdon in Wales, in less than 24 hours.

ELLA'S JOKE

What's black and white, black and white, and black and white?

—

A panda bear rolling down a mountain!

AMY SAYS...

Here are some things to do when out on a long hike:

JUST A MINUTE   Start by choosing someone to be the timer. They can either count down from 60 or time a minute on their phone. Someone chooses a theme (fruit, car parks etc.) then when the timer says so, a different player starts talking about that theme. If they hesitate, stutter or go off track, the other players have to shout out. Whoever challenges first, gets to carry on talking about a different aspect of the subject, and whoever is speaking when the 60 seconds are up, wins a point.

MAKE A STORY   One word at a time. Someone says a starting word (eg 'Once') and then the next person says another word (eg 'Upon'). Carry on this process until you come to the end of the story. There are no rights or wrongs, so no one can say 'that's not right' to someone else — it's all about being creative. Although the story may not go the way you want it to, it may turn out well for other people.

ASSOCIATION – DISASSOCIATION

Say words that are linked with each other in some way. If a word is said and the majority thinks it isn't associated with the other word, the words then are not linked. When a word is said that is linked to another, go back to associated words.

EXPLORING

Getting out into the open air to discover places and activities in your own area or further afield gives you plenty of scope for adventure.

Whether you set out to go caving, foraging or bouldering, or choose to spend a day learning map reading or visiting a local landmark, on foot or by bicycle, you can guarantee an exciting and enjoyable trip.

And there are other options too, such as cooking and eating in the wild, camping at a music festival or walking along an ancient road.

BOULDERING

Go climbing and squeeze between gaps in rocks and boulders – but don't get stuck!

Bouldering, weaselling, canyoning or canyoneering – it's all fancy language for letting kids play on, climb up and squeeze through, gaps in rocks!

This outdoor adventurous play can of course take place on any small rocky outcrop.

Children love to scramble around on rocks and while there is a degree of risk, they generally know their own limits, and play or climb safely within such limits. This means they are assessing potentially dangerous situations and making considered decisions for themselves about risk-taking while keeping themselves safe. Such activities teach children valuable life skills.

Young children, however, should have some degree of supervision and guidance as well as some safety equipment if things get challenging.

For any budding (or experienced) indoor climbers, taking this activity outside adds thrill, adventure and a taste of the 'real' thing.

TIPS AND CONSIDERATIONS

- Youngsters should wear safety helmets when climbing, weaselling and scrambling.
- Gloves should be worn to protect young hands – particularly important when bouldering on rough, igneous rocks like granite.

FIRE STARTING AND COOKING OUTDOORS

Fire starting and cooking adds an extra dimension to any outdoor adventure. Food often seems to taste better when it's cooked and eaten in the fresh air. And a simple meal prepared before, during or after an adventure gives it an expeditionary feel.

Teaching young children how to cook food safely outdoors – knowing when, where and how to light stoves and fires (where appropriate) and safe food storage and cooking, is good preparation for future independent adventuring or travelling.

AMY SAYS...

FOLLOW MY LEADER Create a challenging, but not impossible, route to traverse along. One person starts as the leader and begins to traverse along the route while everyone else follows them. When the leader falls off, they must go to the back of the line and carry on. Keep repeating this until you reach the end of the route. The leader then chooses the next route.

'FAMOUS' ROUTES There are many different paths and cracks in a bouldering wall. Conquer one of the many routes and name it after you, for example 'Katie's Crack of Terror' or 'Craig's Crazy Crevice'. You could also make a map to show all the famous rock marks on the wall. Get creative. It's your place, after all!

DID YOU KNOW?

127 Hours is a biography of a man who gets into difficulty while canyoneering and is trapped for, well, you guessed it, 127 hours!

ELLA'S JOKE

What is a rock's favourite transportation?

—

Rocket!

CAVING

Wrap up well in some waterproofs, helmet and wellies to clamber through a natural cave system.

Caves are natural features that originate from flowing surface water as it makes its way into the ground as a result of gravity's relentless pull. Going underground (where it's usually wet and cold) is not everyone's idea of a good time. Add to it the darkness, the noise of rushing water and pounding waterfalls and it can make the bravest person feel a little nervous (or at the least very respectful of Mother Nature).

Taking kids into caves doesn't have to be (or more importantly shouldn't be) daring or dangerous. There are plenty of 'dry' caves or surface caves to explore initially, and these will be more than thrilling enough for first-time cavers.

For those wanting to venture deeper underground or into a wet cave system, the key to making a trip safe and enjoyable is to rely on local knowledge, appreciate the conditions, and have suitable clothing and equipment.

Wet caving is great fun, even when it's been raining heavily; but take great care to ensure the cave you want to explore is safe. You're likely to see a variety of rocks and fossils like flowstone and limestone. Some of these create strange shapes or patterns, providing proof that they might once have been underwater.

Make sure that you get fully kitted out in waterproof gear, since the flow of water or pools can sometimes be up to knee height.

Caves vary tremendously; not all caves are wet, but the temperature will be different to the outside so it is important to be prepared.

TIPS AND CONSIDERATIONS

- If you are new to caving it is advisable to go with an experienced caver or instructor since they will know the route to navigate and the safety precautions that will need to be taken.
- When entering a surface or dry cave, take a head torch with you and look in nooks and crannies (and on the ceilings) for animal life – you'll be surprised what you may find in the dark underworld.

ELLA'S JOKE

What animal is best at cricket?

—

A bat!

What is the best way to hold a bat?

—

By the bat's handle.

AMY SAYS...

Keep an eye out for natural features such as stalagmites and stalactites. They are long pillars of rock, created over thousands of years, from dripping liquid rock that has solidified. Stalactites hang from the ceiling of the cave (they hold on tight!) and stalagmites rise up from the floor (they use their might to grow!). They are very common in limestone caves and are usually everywhere, so are easy to spot.

NAME GAME Imagine that you are an explorer, looking for features, natural formations or signs of early life (e.g. cave carvings or paintings — although things like that aren't commonly found any more!) When you discover something, remember to give it a name.

DID YOU KNOW?

The longest stalactite ever was around 8m/26ft long!

COOK AND EAT IN THE WILD

More fun than eating in your dining room.

Cooking and eating in the outdoors surrounded by fresh air is a fantastic experience that need not be restricted to summer BBQs or camping expeditions... not when you have a 'tucksack'! A tucksack is a designated rucksack for tuck (food). Find an old rucksack in your garage, loft or shed, grab a camping stove and some simple food to cook, and go 'tucksacking'.

With a tucksack on your back, you can walk, cycle or run to your chosen location and then eat! The location is an important factor. Try to vary where you go and choose places that allow the kids to keep busy and explore.

Once at your chosen outdoor location, get the kids involved. They will love being part of the food preparation, fire starting and cooking in ways they don't have the chance to be at home.

PLACES TO GO TUCKSACKING AND EATING OUT IN THE WILD:

- On a deserted beach.
- On the top of a hill.
- In a cave.
- In a forest.
- On a moor.
- Nestled in a craggy outcrop.
- On the moon (OK, maybe not).

A midweek eat 'out' is a good way to squeeze in an additional dose of family adventure, helping you to maximize the hours between 5pm and 9pm (after school, but back in time for the children's bedtime). You don't need to eat out in restaurants or pubs that entertain the children with 'activity' books. Instead, eat at different outdoor locations and have more fun together, seeing new places, eating healthily and feeling like you have made some progress towards redressing your work/life balance.

AMY SAYS...

Take your skateboard or scooter and play on a skate park while the meal is cooking! This takes your mind off waiting for the food to cook and lets you have more fun. Don't try and do amazing stunts unless you know what you're doing — you could really hurt yourself!

Pack binoculars or a telescope and do some stargazing. If you aren't really one for whizzing round on scooters or bikes, or are in the wrong location, it's also fun to look at the stars and identify them. Look for things like Orion's nebulae.

Play on a playground or outdoor gym while waiting for your meal — this gets you fit and is fun to do!

DID YOU KNOW?

Spending more time outdoors is better for you; it's been proven that it makes you healthier and happier.

ELLA'S JOKE

Knock, knock.
Who's there?
Lettuce
Lettuce who?
Lettuce in, we're freezing!

(DON'T) FOLLOW A PATH

Go off-road hiking and avoid the crowds.

Leave the path – especially if it's a crowded one – and go for a scramble!

This adventure comes into its own when you are pretty familiar with the terrain and location, because it's a bit like going off-piste when skiing or snowboarding – except you are going uphill, not downhill!

Starting the adventure is all about finding an alternative route to the summit of a hill or small mountain. The thing is, if you know where you are heading (the familar bit), you can be a little more adventurous with the route you take to get there. This is especially rewarding when the regular path is crowded with people, so use this as motivation to do an off-path scramble.

The first time we did this it was when a path was annoyingly busy – mainly due to slow people who were inadequately prepared for the outdoors. One person was even wearing leather boots with pointy heels! We jumped on a remark made by our youngest ... 'Let's go this way...' (pointing straight up the side of the hill). A few astonished faces later, we were off. We had the hillside to ourselves and our hearts were pounding due to the gradient and the feeling of adventure and excitement! The view was great – so too was seeing the faces of people below watching two young children scrambling up the hillside, squealing with delight as they clambered up.

So next time you are out walking and feel the need for a bit of adventure, encourage your children to lead the (alternative) way!

TIPS AND CONSIDERATIONS

- Always respect the local environment and be careful not to cause harm or damage to the land, animals or people.
- Wear sturdy shoes to avoid twisted ankles.
- Be aware of what is below you – you don't want any rocks or stones falling on unsuspecting walkers below.
- Don't walk 'off-path' in areas of conservation, particularly where there are signs asking you to stick to paths in order to avoid erosion.

AMY SAYS...

Talk to the animals. Whenever you see wild animals such as grazing sheep, cows etc., try to get a conversation going with them by speaking to them in their 'language'. Try out different types of 'baas' or 'moos' and see what reactions you get. See who is worthy enough to claim the title Dr Doolittle.

DID YOU KNOW?

Paths are eroded (worn away) by the walkers who travel along them.

ELLA'S JOKE

What do you call
a dinosaur that smashes
everything in its path?
—
Tyrannosaurus wrecks!

EXPLORE AN ABANDONED RUIN

Visit a location where you can discover ruined buildings or abandoned wrecks.

A trip to an old aeroplane crash site, shipwreck or ruined historical building will engage even the most reluctant young walker to take on the idea of a six- or seven-mile hike in order to get there. Obviously, the more dramatic, mysterious and exciting the better – that way you can encourage a youngster to endure an even longer walk to reach the destination. The trek or walk to the site is as much part of the adventure as the location itself.

There are many aeroplane crash sites littered across mountains and hills around the world, leftover reminders of the destruction and carnage of war (although crashes do occur accidentally during peacetime too, of course.) If you search online for a site near to where you live, you'll be able to find something interesting, exciting (perhaps with landing gear and other structural wreckage) and poignant (with a makeshift or formal memorial in situ). History doesn't get more tangible and real than this.

A shipwreck on a beach could reward an exploring beach trekker. Shipwrecks aren't often documented sites, so most are heard of by word of mouth or local knowledge. The state of the ship needs to be considered before exploring it. When at the site, document some details, then when you return home you could find out any relevant information linked to it.

Encourage children to take on the role of investigators; they could estimate the size of the original ship by pacing out the dimensions and also work out how old it is according to how many barnacles etc. are on it.

Other sites to visit could include castle sites or other mediaeval ruins, the less known the better. Stone circles or the ruined remains of an ancient village might also stimulate the imagination.

AMY SAYS...

Come up with exciting headlines that might describe what happened at the site. Think about what happened, when it happened and who was involved. Try and make the headlines snappy, exciting and attention-grabbing.

DID YOU KNOW?

An American fighter plane, named 'Over Exposed', crashed near Snake Pass in the Peak District and the parts of it are still there today.

ELLA'S JOKE

An archeologist is a
person whose career
lies in *ruins*!

FAMILY ORIENTEERING

Work as a family to navigate an orienteering course.

Orienteering is a sport that requires navigation around an area using a map to find specific points, usually against other competitors. It doesn't have to be serious or competitive though, and makes for a fun and lively activity.

Many forest parks you may have visited before are likely to have a trail of some kind to follow, but it's worth asking at the site's information centre to see if they have a proper orienteering trail.

For some, the term orienteering might sound a bit 'serious' or perhaps a bit technical, but actually it simply involves following a pre-set course and finding marker posts. Family orienteering courses will be quite easy to follow, and often themed to appeal to the youngest of orienteerers. Contact local forest parks or tourism centres to find a suitable place to try orienteering.

Trails aimed at older or more serious participants will provide a map that is quite similar to a normal walkers' map, but it will be printed to an appropriate scale, with the markers that need to be found numbered and marked on the map.

Consider joining a local 'fun day' organized by a local orienteering club. There will be different courses and distances to complete.

TIPS AND CONSIDERATIONS

- Introduce the notion of orienteering in your own garden. Make pictorial maps and set treasure trails for young children to complete as a fun way to learn.
- Orienteering is hungry and thirsty work; take plenty of snacks and drinks with you and regularly replenish your youngster's energy and hydration levels.
- If you are trying orienteering as a family, you might want to split into teams and add an element of competition; half the group completes the course in a clockwise direction, with the others working in an anti-clockwise direction. It adds an element of excitement and urgency – and extra fun.

BENEFITS OF ORIENTEERING

- Develops spatial awareness.
- Offers a great opportunity to develop map-reading and navigational skills.
- Improves fitness and well-being; running around a forest is great psychological therapy. It's a 'crafty' way to build up children's fitness levels and perseverance because when focused and motivated to complete the trail, they won't even notice the distances they are covering.
- A great family activity that costs next to nothing.

AMY SAYS...

COMPASS BEARING CHALLENGE

Someone chooses an object quite nearby and shares
its location with whoever has the compass. That person
then has to take a bearing of the object by pointing the
compass's direction of travel arrow towards the chosen
object. They then line up the red 'floating' needle
with the red orienting arrow by rotating the bezel.
The number on the outside of the bezel (0 to 360)
is the bearing of the object. Players swap over.

ELLA'S JOKE

What's big, white, furry
and always points North?

—

A Polar bearing.

DID YOU KNOW?

Orienteering was first
founded in the late
19th century in Sweden.

FORAGE FOR FOOD

Cook with food that you've found and freshly picked.

There's something very rewarding about eating for free... no, we don't mean having a meal and then not paying for it, but rather growing and eating a healthy meal fresh from Mother Nature's pantry.

Instead of sitting at home or at a restaurant, find a picturesque setting outdoors for a meal. And instead of rummaging through ingredients in the kitchen cupboard and taking everything with you, why not supplement your meal by foraging for fruit, vegetables or herbs found growing naturally in the outdoors?

There are plenty of ingredients out there in the wild that can be added to a tasty meal. A large part of the fun is foraging for them. Children love exploring the outdoors; they'll soon build up an appetite searching for and choosing the ingredients for the meal that they will be making and eating.

Throughout the year it is possible to find an abundance of fruit such as brambles, strawberries, raspberries, apples, plums, and pears etc. Many people collect fruit and take it home to make pies or crumbles, but it seems a shame not to enjoy the natural setting for longer, so stay on and eat in the place where the ingredients were collected.

BREAKFAST COMPÔTE

Get up early one morning and go out for breakfast. It could even be a stop-off en-route to somewhere else. Collect some berries, give them a wash and stew them with some sugar to make a compôte. Cook up some porridge then add the compôte for a tasty, healthy and fun family breakfast. Everyone is involved in the process and the reward is a good one!

AMY SAYS...

Great tips for when you're making nettle soup: add lots of potatoes and try not to look at the colour when you're eating it! It looks yucky, but tastes really nice.

BERRIES They're just the right colour for fake blood! Grab a few, crush and spread the juice around a patch of skin. Then run to your parents, screaming that you've hurt yourself. If your acting is good enough, they'll be easily tricked!

DIY BERRY BALL It's like paint balling but stepped up a gear. Take an old t-shirt or hoodie and old trousers for this activity to avoid staining any new clothes.
Fill some old bits of thin cloth with mushy berries or over-ripe brambles etc. and throw them at another opponent who is also wearing old clothing. It's great fun!

NETTLE SOUP

You may think that getting children to pick, never mind eat, nettles seems destined to failure (after all, getting them to eat mange tout or green beans is hard enough isn't it). But, you may be surprised at how well your children rise to the challenge and there's only one way to find out...

- Put on a pair of gardening gloves (rubber kitchen gloves are the best).
- Pick a bag full of nettle tops (the young growth at the top of the stem).
- Rinse the nettle tops and remove any thick stems / tough pieces.
- Boil some potatoes.
- Add some garlic (wild garlic preferably) and the nettles.
- Blend the potatoes, nettles and garlic.
- Add some stock into the blended mix and simmer.
- Serve with a swirl of yoghurt or crème fraîche.
- Season, then eat with crusty bread.

DID YOU KNOW?

It's actually the hairs on nettles that sting you!

ELLA'S JOKE

Why was the blackberry sad?
—
Because her mum was in a jam!

GEOCACHING

Go on a treasure hunt using GPS.

Anyone who enjoys treasure hunts will love geocaching. This family activity encourages working as a team to explore an area in search of treasure spots (geocaches). Despite its simplicity, geocaching is a valuable, educational and fun activity, requiring useful skills such as map reading, navigation and observational skills on top of the thrill and excitement of a treasure hunt. Oh and not forgetting plenty of fresh air and exercise of course!

Geocaches can be found all over, from unusual remote locations to surprising spots right under your nose, hidden in the crack of a wall in a city centre for example! A geocache usually consists of a camouflaged plastic tub (sizes differ) with random 'prizes' – usually small plastic toys – placed inside. Caches include a notepad in which you are encouraged to write the date, your name and a comment. Their locations are graded according to how hard they are to find.

Very little equipment is needed to take part; you do not need an expensive GPS tool since a 'smart' phone with data allowance is more than sufficient for the beginner. You need to download a geocaching app and log on to a geocaching website, where you'll then be able to locate your area.

When you set out in search of a geocache, you should take your phone with you. Keep referring to the map as you plan and follow your chosen route. Once in the vicinity of the 'treasure' you'll need two things – the reference point and keen eyesight!

If and when you find the geocache take a look inside. You may remove an item from the box and add your own contribution. Don't forget to sign and date the notebook and remember to read the other comments by fellow geocachers.

TIPS AND CONSIDERATIONS

- Be prepared to clamber over rocks and through bushes in the more remote locations.
- Take a small item to put into the geocache, replacing the item that you take out. Do not take any food items since, for obvious reasons, they might decay before someone finds them.

AMY SAYS...

Geocaching is a super high-tech treasure hunt. Start at an easy level, then work your way up to more difficult caches as you become experts.

When you find the location, don't let your parents find the cache — they'll try to take the glory but that's your job!

Some of the toys in the cache can be a little disappointing so try to be creative and make it interesting for the next person — what would you want to find? You could create a little treasure map or set of instructions for someone to find that will lead them to your treat.

DID YOU KNOW?

People that are not involved in geocaching are referred to as 'muggles'.

ELLA'S JOKE

What did the pirate do before he buried his treasure?

—

Dug a hole.

GO FOR A REPTILE RAMBLE

Spot some native lizards and snakes in their natural habitat.

This is a walk taken at a much slower than normal pace, with the intention of spotting lizards and snakes in their natural environments.

Spotting snakes and lizards is one thing, but knowing what type they are is a different skill, so it pays to do a little research before you head out (or get yourself a beginner's spotter guide). You will then have a clear idea of what to look for when out walking.

TIPS AND CONSIDERATIONS

- The best time to spot lizards is in the early morning or on warmer, sunnier days when they are likely to be sunbathing on rocks.
- Walk (or creep) slowly and carefully – lizards and snakes will detect any vibrations.
- Be very careful when looking for snakes with your children, particularly adders.
- Remember to be patient and don't give up if you don't see any on your first outing.

AMY SAYS...

LOOK OUT FOR OTHER WILDLIFE

Take your time and keep your eyes peeled for other wildlife when you are looking for snakes and lizards, as you are certain to see beautifully coloured butterflies and mini-beasts such as beetles, spiders and flying bugs too.

SNAKES

Grass snakes

- Quite common, especially near water.
- Light green in colour, with black marks down the sides.

Adders

- Found on moorland, in woodlands and often on disused (or quiet) railway embankments.
- Have a line of triangular shapes running down their backs.
- Females are brown and males are a greyish colour with black markings.

Did you know adders give birth to live young?

NB *Adders are venomous, so take care not to startle or corner them.*

Smooth snakes

- Less common than grass snakes and adders.
- They are a browny-green colour.

LIZARDS

Slow worms

- Legless lizard, often mistaken for a snake.
- Grey/brown colour with shiny-looking scales.
- Females have a black stripe and dark sides.
- Males sometimes have blue spots.

COMMON LIZARDS

- Vary in colour from brown to yellow or green.
- Often have spots or stripes along the back or sides.

Sand lizard

- More rare but can be found in sandy heathland in the south of England.
- Brownish with dark and light patterns and two black stripes.
- During the mating season, male sand lizards have bright green sides.

DID YOU KNOW?

Smooth snakes are an endangered species and you need a special licence to handle them.

ELLA'S JOKE

What is a snake's favourite subject?
—
Hissss-tory!

Why did the snake laugh so hard she started to cry?
—
She thought the joke was hissss-terical!

HIKE AND CAMP

Challenge yourself to a longer hike, with an overnight camp-out along the way.

Who says you need to end a walk and return home to the comfort of your own bed? This challenge combines hiking a fair distance with camping out in the wild for a night.

It is a good idea to have an idea of how far you wish to walk and where you will set up camp. The age and ability of family members will dictate a suitable length, gradient and therefore location. Take plenty of liquids and snacks to keep up the energy levels and then enjoy plodding, strolling, ambling and trudging across the countryside, appreciating the views and chatting along the way.

Plan your walk accordingly; with young children you'll have to carry most of the sleeping, cooking and eating equipment so pack lightly. Small, light sachets of soup and cereal or porridge packets take up little space

and provide a nutritious meal before and after sleeping; a small camping stove and kettle will be all that's needed. The only other consideration is sleeping bags, roll mats and tents or bivvi bags plus layers of clothing for warmth once the sun goes down. This is when size matters, so ideally take smaller sleeping bags with you as they take up less space. Bivvi bags also pack up small and are quick to set up.

To truly escape from the world, find a secluded location that has a beautiful view to wake up to. Don't forget you'll have to walk back the next day.

AMY SAYS...

Have a themed conversation. Choose a theme (e.g. a book or a film) and see how many references you can make to it in your conversation.

Example topic: *Star Wars*
Luke over there. I'm getting cold —
I'll put another *Leia* on!

TIPS AND CONSIDERATIONS

- Travel light. Encourage the children, depending on their age and size, to carry some of the load.
- Take some wet bags (or carrier bags) to store shoes, camera and any electrical equipment in; even if it doesn't rain, things can get damp in the morning dew.
- Be prepared for all weathers.

DID YOU KNOW?

Hiking is known as 'hill walking' in the UK; 'bush walking' in Australia; 'tramping' in New Zealand and 'trekking' in India and Africa.

ELLA'S JOKE

Two sisters are out hiking.
The first sister asks,
'Did you see that?'
'No.' the second sister replies.
'Well, an eagle just flew overhead.'
the first sister says.
'Oh.' says the second sister.
A couple of minutes later,
the first sister asks,
'Did you see that?'
'See what?' the second sister replies.
'Are you blind? There was a red deer
on that hill, over there.'
'Oh.'
A few minutes later, the first sister asks,
'Did you see that?'
By now, the second sister is getting
aggravated, so she says,
'Yes, of course I did!'
And the first sister says,
'Then why did you step in it?'

CHILDREN-LED ADVENTURE

Let the kids choose where to walk to and how to get there (using a map of course).

You don't have to go far to experience an adventure nor do you even need a vehicle; you just need to step out of your front door, take a walk and explore!

This adventure is simple, but also important for instilling some key skills in your children. The kids need to experience the planning and preparation for a trip; thinking about the scenarios they may encounter, the weather conditions and the necessary equipment. Set them the challenge of organizing a local hike that goes from door to door and covers a specific distance.

Give the children a map of the local area and a map measurer (if you have one) and ask them to find a route that starts from your house, goes around the surrounding streets and further afield, and fits your ideal mileage. Once they've planned the route, ask them to pack the bags and set off – whatever the weather. Since the children have planned the route, they also need to lead it, by reading a map. This should provide plenty of opportunity to talk about how to read a map, calculate distances and spot landmarks. There's no need to worry about getting lost, because you're really not too far from home.

Hopefully, even though you are familiar with your own area, you'll be surprised to find unusual and interesting places that you've never seen before or you have previously overlooked due to the everyday hustle and bustle of life.

TIPS AND CONSIDERATIONS

- Take a picnic and snacks – hungry walkers can be grumpy ones!
- Take a tarpaulin or shelter to provide cover for the picnic. The kids can make the sandwiches or plan the one-pot supper!

ELLA'S JOKE

Three siblings planned a trip to go on a picnic. When they got there, they realized they'd forgotten the fizzy pop. The youngest sibling said he would go home and get it, as long as they wouldn't eat the sandwiches until he got back. A week went by, then a month, finally a year, when the two siblings said, 'Oh, come on, let's eat the sandwiches.' Suddenly the little sibling popped up from behind a rock and said, 'If you do, I won't go!'

AMY SAYS...

This is our chance to take charge! Plan an adventure that will take the adults out of their comfort zone and see where you end up.

While you're trudging through fields or tramping along pavements, have a few games up your sleeve to keep the folks entertained:

- Go alphabet exploring. Try to spot different things that start with each letter of the alphabet.
- Look out for silly signs that tell you to do things then do them! For example at the 'Lotto – Play Here' sign, stand and play any game you like for a few minutes.

DID YOU KNOW?

Dave Cornthwaite, a British adventurer, is attempting to complete 25 journeys of 1000 miles or more, each using a different form of non-motorized transport.

LEARN MAP-READING SKILLS

As sat-navs and GPS systems become commonplace, the need for map reading is not relied on in the same way as it once was – especially when driving. But for anyone who spends time walking in the outdoors, the ability to understand and accurately follow a map can be more than useful; it could potentially be a lifesaver.

Map reading – or more accurately exposure to maps – can start at an early age. Once children understand the concept of a 'bird's eye view' they can begin making and following plans and maps of some sort. Extend this awareness of maps to the real world when out walking and adventuring, by always making sure you have a map of the area with the route you are following.

As children get older, help them interpret the maps you are using. Encourage and support them to look for features on the map in the real world e.g. a path, track, wall or stream. Children love to take the lead when you're out and about, and usually enjoy the responsibility of being group leader. Give them control of the map and let them lead the way – what is the worst that can happen? OK, you will need to keep a subtle eye on things, but the more practice the young map readers have, the better they will become.

Any activity on map reading has to include compass points. Knowledge of the compass points is important, as is the ability to read and set bearings, but these are skills that can be mastered once a child has gained a good grasp of map reading. An appreciation of the scale of a map is also an important concept that can be made at a later date. Don't rush children; let them consolidate their map-reading skills in a fun and non-threatening environment.

TIPS AND CONSIDERATIONS

- Always carry a map if you can. Demonstrate the use of a map to explain the value of carrying, and being able to read one.
- Read a map out loud so everyone can hear, and be aware of, next movements.
- Use maps of different scales to match your type of walk.
- Protect your maps by using a waterproof map case.

AMY SAYS...

Convince the adults to let you take the lead on a walk as often as possible. Ask them to keep a bit of an eye on where you are going though — especially if you are not so confident — just so you don't end up leading them anywhere unsafe or undesirable!

Make your own map when you get back after the walk. Include all of the details you can, and add little sketches and doodles to make it more interesting.

DID YOU KNOW?

In the past, mapmakers included fake towns (or 'paper towns') on their maps so they could catch out forgers.

ELLA'S JOKE

Why was the map gesturing wildly?
—
It was an animated map.

MUSIC FESTIVAL

Depending on which country you are in when you go to a music festival, some may have a reputation for being wet and muddy affairs. The poor weather conditions and muddy frolicking often steal the limelight at the expense of the music. But there are also a lot of other factors and activities that are capable of turning a music festival into a rich family adventure.

Absorb the atmosphere

There will be lots going on that you can get involved with. Encourage your young ones to watch the entertainer, take part in the arts and crafts, dance around to the music and, most of all, have fun.

Explain the notion of multi-cultural life

There will be lots of cultural and ethnic representations. Embrace these and help youngsters value and appreciate the richness of diverse cultures.

Encourage open-mindedness

Before you set off, make an informal pact to try new things together: listen to new music, try new foods, take part in new activities. An open mind and a 'give-it-a-go' attitude will lead to new opportunities in life, so use the festival occasion to help nurture this.

Let go of your inhibitions

Not that you should ever need it, but it goes without saying that attending a festival gives you 'permission' to let your hair down.

TIPS AND CONSIDERATIONS

- Take some food and drink with you. Enjoy the variety of foods on offer at the stalls, but take additional snacks of your own to help keep costs down.
- Take sunscreen and apply it regularly, if you're lucky enough to have sunshine!
- Be prepared for the weather: take spare clothes and something to sit on.
- Go through the 'I'm lost' protocol and have an agreed meeting point.
- Safety in crowds: beware of pickpockets and the behaviour of others who may possibly be under the influence of alcohol.
- Explicit language warning: unfortunately, some bands feel they have to swear a lot when playing live.

ELLA'S JOKE

What do you call a cow that
plays an instrument?

—

A Moo-sician!

AMY SAYS...

There is often a range of arts and crafts on
offer at festivals, including the opportunity
to learn circus skills. Have a go; try to learn
how to juggle, spin plates or walk on stilts.

A trendy thing to do is decorate your face
and arms with body paints. You can buy
some there or take some with you.

DID YOU KNOW?

The Glastonbury festival in Somerset,
UK uses about 300 megawatts of
electricity in one weekend. The same
amount that can power a small city!

SAMPLE BACKPACKING

Carry everything you need in a backpack and go off on an adventure.

As soon as your children are old enough, big enough and strong enough to carry their own backpack, they are ready to be introduced to backpacking – or even 'Inter-Railing'. Of course, the first step is probably not going to involve catching trains across Europe, but giving children early exposure to the idea of 'travelling light' with only a rucksack on their back, will no doubt lead to longer, more adventurous travels in the future.

This isn't to underestimate the value of a short backpacking expedition within your own country.

MAKE A BACKPACKING CITY TRIP MORE EXCITING AND ADVENTUROUS

- Give your children the responsibility of being group leaders.
- Deliberately book rail journeys that involve a change (or two) – this really makes it feel like you are on a 'proper' journey.
- Encourage your children to look for platform numbers and departure/arrival time displays.
- Make sure your children know where they are going... geographically, that is. Get out a map and show children the rail route you are taking. It's bound to be different to a road route (discuss the reasons for this).
- Encourage children to communicate with rail staff, bus drivers etc. – it's a valuable opportunity to help your children develop key communication skills.

THINGS TO REMEMBER

A lot of 'adventurous' activities you embark on with your children are all about instilling and developing a positive mindset towards challenge, adventure and opportunities. The more actively engaged they are with planning, packing and communicating, the deeper their experience. Get used to stepping back and relinquishing control. What is the worst that can happen?

AMY SAYS...

TAKE CHARGE This is a great chance for us kids to dictate and tell the adults where we want to go. Museums, playgrounds and village gardens are some of the places kids want to visit so why, when an opportunity like this arises, should we not go? It's still exploring, right?

Living out of a small rucksack is a good excuse for being a bit lazy — try travelling light. A drink, some snacks, maybe some spending money and a change of clothes or an extra sweater is all that's needed!

PLAY CARD GAMES ON TRAINS It's not so easy in a car, but sat around a table on a train is a different story. Card games are super easy to play as long as the train isn't on a bumpy path that sends the cards scattering round the carriage!

DID YOU KNOW?

Forty per cent of backpackers choose to go to Europe for their shorter trips!

ELLA'S JOKE

RULES OF RUCKSACK

1 No matter how carefully you pack, a rucksack is always too small.
2 No matter how small, a rucksack is always too heavy.
3 No matter how heavy, a rucksack will never contain what you want.
4 No matter what you need, it's always at the bottom of your rucksack.

SEE A HENGE OR ANCIENT SITE
FROM SUNSET TO SUNRISE

Find a local stone-age works for the summer solstice and spend the night nearby.

This adventure is all about getting outdoors in the summer time and enjoying the delights of an evening sunset, the thrill of open-air camping (bivvi bagging) and the excitement of an early morning sunrise. It really is that simple.

A popular time to complete this adventure with other people is midsummer, or the summer solstice. This is a time when the earth is most inclined towards the sun. The solstice day, as it is called, is the one day of the year that has the most daylight hours.

Engage children's interest by joining in with a summer solstice celebration. Countries all around the world celebrate this day with a festival or holiday, and participation usually involves dressing up and singing songs.

Alternatively, if you are not keen on joining in with some ancient ritual, find an atmospheric setting of your own for this adventure – the surroundings and ambience will see your location take on an inspiring magical form!

The winter solstice is often celebrated and acknowledged too. It occurs on the shortest day of the year, but as it falls during winter you might not be so keen to spend it outdoors!

TIPS AND CONSIDERATIONS

- Look online for celebrations and local customs that you can learn about, and join in with.
- Respect the area in which you celebrate an equinox; henges, burial sites and monument sites are often full of heritage and history so leave them as you find them.

AMY SAYS...

Create a tale about how the henge you visited got there — there are all sorts of stories on how stone circles were built and how, so why not make up your own about the place you visited. It can be as creative as you want — in fact, the more creative the better. Think about the shapes of the place you visited and why they were like that. Maybe you could even research about the culture of the people who you believe built the site?

ELLA'S JOKE

I was walking round Stonehenge the other day when I noticed a boy smiling at me from the other side. There must have been some sort of attraction between us.

DID YOU KNOW?

Stonehenge in Wiltshire attracts over one million visitors each year.

SLEEP IN A HOMEMADE SHELTER

Make your own shelter from branches, twigs and leaves, then sleep in it.

There is certainly something primitive in knowing how to build a shelter, but also something comforting in knowing that, if necessary, one could make an emergency dwelling in which to shelter or hide.

Shelter building, as an organized or independent collaborative family challenge is a fun but valuable learning experience, and the stakes seem so much higher when you know the shelter you build will be the only thing between you and the elements. This really focuses the mind. Building a shelter out of branches, sticks and bracken is just one aspect of this outdoor learning experience.

At organized shelter-building events children and adults may learn (or re-learn) the skills associated with starting and sustaining an outdoor fire, as well as how to cook on it and, most importantly, how to safely extinguish it. As adults we can all probably remember 'playing' with fire as children. But how often do today's children experience such powerful play?

Sleeping in a 'made by me' shelter can be an amazing experience. The fresh air (and midges) on your face and the sounds of the forest alive with nightlife is a thrill. You may even be so lucky to have deer visit your camp during the night! OK, so you may not sleep so well, but that won't matter. After all, who wants to sleep through an exciting night under stars with minibeasts and larger wildlife?

TIPS AND CONSIDERATIONS

- Encourage and support children's natural den-making activities from a young age. Let them find branches and twigs, and offer assistance with how to organize them into a simple structure.
- Older or more experienced den builders can be introduced to some of the basic shelter designs – search the internet for instructions and examples.
- By far the hardest part of building a shelter is making it resistant to rain. Lots of foliage, organized layer upon layer, will be required to keep moisture out. A good test is to lie in the shelter and look for any daylight gaps in your structure.
- If you are planning to sleep out in your shelter, consider using a tarpaulin too. It's a bit of a cheat, but at least you'll stay dry.

DID YOU KNOW?

A healthy human can survive for several weeks without food, and several days without water, but in many cases only several hours without proper shelter from the weather.

ELLA'S JOKE

How does a penguin build its house?
—
Igloos it together!

AMY SAYS...

BUILD A SHELTER FOR INSECTS Find some old twigs and bracken or moss and pile them all up as a shelter. Make it look as hidden as possible, away from people or predators. It doesn't have to be neat — the bugs won't really mind! As long as it's dark and safe, it is perfect for the critters who take refuge in it on a wet day.

SLEEP IN AN ECO TENT

Try sleeping in an eco tent, which is a new alternative to the traditional tent and is an increasingly popular offering at campsites.

If you feel the need for some 'glamping' then an eco tent might be the thing to try. If nothing else, it offers a different and quite cosy experience, with everyone sharing bunk beds in a single room.

The term 'eco tent' can be a bit ambiguous and open to interpretation, meaning different things to different people and providers. In essence it is a no-frills hut or shed, fitted with simple facilities such as bunk beds, an eating area and occasionally electric lighting and powered sockets. Cooking and washing facilities are shared in a communal building, as are modern conveniences such as a fridge.

Bedding-wise, all that guests need to bring with them are sleeping bags and pillows.

Due to the basic nature of eco tents, they tend to be quite reasonably priced if you shop around. Having said that, compared to some of the tents you see on some sites these days (with extensions, electric hook-ups and even satellite TV), eco tenting is actually far less glamorous and feels rough and ready, so is still a real adventure.

One advantage of eco tents is that they extend the camping season well into the colder months. You could actually spend a comfortable night in an eco-tent all year round (assuming sites are open, of course).

So, next time you fancy a night under canvas, consider leaving the tent in the garage and go 'eco tenting' for an alternative and spontaneous get-away night.

TIPS AND CONSIDERATIONS

- Book an eco-tent if you want a night away from the house when the weather might be a little on the cold side for canvas camping.
- Off-peak times will be less busy, so booking may not be required, which makes a trip more spontaneous.
- If you're looking for a true 'eco' experience, hunt around on the internet for providers who offer carbon-neutral camping.

ELLA'S JOKE

What do you call a
sleeping dinosaur?
—
A dino-snore!

AMY SAYS...

Organize games for everyone to play.
Team games are much better when
played with plenty of people. Rounders,
soccer, cricket or softball are all good
games to play.

Take control of meal times. You're not
cooking on a stove in an eco tent, so
your options are more open. Why don't
you make a meal? When camping, a
meal needs to be made quickly so it
keeps warm, and has to be easy to
make (for these reasons the adults
usually make the meal). But in an eco
tent you're under shelter and are
keeping warmer than normal, so more
complicated meals can be made — and
made by you. Be creative but not
unrealistic — things like huge desserts
aren't really appropriate.

DID YOU KNOW?

Something called a
solar-powered tent was
created to celebrate the
Glastonbury festival and
is powered by sunlight
so that 'glampers' can
keep in touch with
friends via phones etc.

TAG TEAM CYCLE TRAIL

Complete a long cycle ride by breaking it down into stages.

Having a young family doesn't mean you can't embark on lengthy, challenging cycle rides or trails; especially not if you attempt a challenging ride as a family tag-team!

The idea is to find a cycle route that would be too long and challenging for your young children to complete in full on their own, then break the ride down into manageable chunks, splitting the family into teams and taking it in turns to take on roles by cycling the route and providing support to each of the cyclists in the team.

Each child or group of children should take it in turns to ride each of the 'chunks' (accompanined by an adult of course), making completion of the route manageable as they are part of the tag-team. The support team drives to designated meeting points, carrying the essential bike rack and nutritional supplies. The child(ren) within the support team can then map-read and track the route that both cyclists and the support vehicle are taking.

The sense of fulfilment and achievement for children at the end of the cycle challenge is strong... and made more so by the fact that they have worked as part of a team towards competing a shared goal. This in itself is valuable learning. And there are of course

the obvious benefits of exercise, the experience of needing a positive, optimistic attitude, as well as recognizing and valuing others' efforts and the need for teamwork.

TIPS AND CONSIDERATIONS

- Remember, this activity is as much about attitude-forming skills as it is about the challenge itself.
- As soon as your youngest rider can use a balance bike, try this adventure.
- Use language in a way that supports and encourages the effort as much as it praises the end result.
- Look for local trails and cycle routes that are not next to roads or traffic. Old disused railways make good locations.
- Insist that riders wear helmets at all times and are aware of others on the trail, especially faster riders who come up from behind.

DID YOU KNOW?

Modern bicycle design is based on a draisine, which was two-wheeled and invented by a German called Baron Karl Von Drais in 1817.

AMY SAYS...

Be prepared to swallow a fly or two while cycling — you're more than likely to, especially if you're a chatterbox! Don't worry, the chances are it will probably be a giant bluebottle, not a midge!

RING YOUR BELL Enjoy the power you have to clear a path of pedestrians by giving a loud ring as you are approaching. Try to avoid crashing. If they don't move out of the way, don't ram into them, simply go around them. However, if a racing cyclist or a group of cyclists is coming your way or trying to overtake, don't try to block them or force them to move.

ELLA'S JOKE

What is the difference between a nicely-dressed man on a tricycle and a poorly dressed man on a bicycle?

—

Attire!

TRACK AND CAST ANIMAL FOOTPRINTS

Find animal footprints when out on a walk and make casts using plaster of Paris.

When the forest is wet, muddy and squidgy underfoot, gather together some plaster of Paris, cardboard strips, paper clips and water, then go in search of animal footprints.

Search for prints on paths or glades, or anywhere that you can see patches of soft mud. When you find a print, identify it using a footprints guide of some kind; there are lots to be found online. Or, if you have a smart phone or iTouch, take a photograph to give you a handy interactive and pocket-sized digital identification guide.

TIPS AND CONSIDERATIONS

- Make sure children know that they should avoid getting the plaster mixture on their hands. If they do, it should be washed off immediately.
- Take plenty of plaster of Paris and water with you – this allows for some mistakes to be made.

ELLA'S JOKE

How do you know if there's a dinosaur in your refrigerator?
—
Look for footprints in the pizza!

DID YOU KNOW?

Apart from making footprint casts, plaster of Paris has many other uses, such as sculpture (art and architecture) and holding bones together (medicine).

HOW TO MAKE A CAST OF A FOOTPRINT

Use a cardboard strip (and some paper clips) to make a 'bracelet'. Push the cardboard into the ground so that it surrounds the footprint.

Mix the plaster of Paris with some water until it is not too thick, but not too thin (the thicker it is, the quicker it will dry BUT if it's too thick, it won't flow into the print well enough).

Pour or scoop the mix into the footprint then smooth if off with the back of a spoon.

Leave for about 30-60 minutes ... or until you think the plaster has hardened enough. This will depend on:
- The thickness (depth) of your cast.
- How thick (gloopy) your plaster mix was.
- The weather conditions.

Carefully unfasten the paper clips and peel apart the cardboard bracelet. Gently does it, because the plaster is still fragile (and the plaster that is in contact with the soil may still be drying).

If the cast comes out looking dirty, with mud attached, don't worry – this is normal. When the cast has been given time to fully harden (about two hours), the mud and dirt will brush off, leaving a nice clean footprint cast.

AMY SAYS...

You can make casts of anything: your footprint, a plastic toy or your pet dog's paw print. Find a place that is muddy, but where the mud hasn't been disturbed, to make the print or go searching for another animal's print in the woods. A deer or rabbit print would be good.

While waiting for your cast to set, use some sticks and twigs to make a protective guard around it and to make people even more aware of it. Make it like a castle's walls by sinking sticks into the floor around it.

When your cast is ready, paint and varnish it to make it stand out.

VISIT A LANDMARK

Travel to a well-known natural or manmade landmark and marvel at its intricate and inventive method of construction.

This is a simple adventure for any time of the year, but perfect for when you are on holiday or perhaps visiting a different part of the country, or the world.

Visiting a large-scale landmark can be exciting and exhilarating for children. And there are plenty to visit, explore and learn about – whether it's contemporary art, local history or an ancient relic. There will always be a human story behind an artefact. Natural formations will also delight an enquiring mind, and have the added interest of human relationships connected to them as well.

Try and get to know the stories or history behind the places you visit, and share this knowledge with your family members. It promotes and values curiosity and inquiry; important skills to try and nurture within children from a young age.

The same applies to naturally formed landmarks; there will most likely be a geographical story behind each one you visit. Once understood, these stories will give youngsters a greater understanding of the world they live in.

HERE ARE SOME IDEAS FOR UK LANDMARKS TO VISIT:

- Hadrian's Wall
- The White Horse of Kilburn
- The Angel of the North
- Stonehenge

Other ideas include:
- Castles and forts.
- Cliffs and stacks.
- Valleys and canyons.
- Ancient monuments and settlements.
- Religious statues and shrines.

AMY SAYS...

KICK A BALL AROUND A LANDMARK

Kicking a ball around a landmark is great exercise. Not only is it good for your body, but also it lets you see different angles of the landmark; views of things you might never have seen before if you had not done it this way. It doesn't have to be a big famous landmark like the Eiffel Tower or the Leaning Tower of Pisa. It could just be a local monument or place, or even a famous tree!

MAKE A SHORT NEWS REPORT

Try compiling a report on the story behind a monument, natural formation or iconic landmark. The information you need may be shown at the landmark itself or you may have to search the internet to find out more.

Visit a landmark that ties in with school work — it will make completing homework or a study project more fun and meaningful.

ELLA'S JOKE

I heard you slipped while climbing up a tower in Paris.

—

Eiffel!

DID YOU KNOW?

Buckingham Palace has 775 known rooms. These include 19 state rooms, 52 royal and guest bedrooms, 188 staff bedrooms, 92 offices and 78 bathrooms!

WALK AN ANCIENT ROAD

Find an ancient Roman road and... just keep on walking.

Walking along a road might not sound very appealing, in fact walking along a straight ancient road could sound quite boring. However, with a bit of imagination you may find that following in the footsteps of historical figures can be an adventure. The ancient road will dictate where you walk; it might be a small section of the whole walk or the main route that you follow.

Many ancient roads are now in ruins or covered by modern tarmac, but with a bit of research you should be able to find walks that follow the route that an ancient road would once have taken. If you're lucky there may

even be remnants of stones or cobbled paths along the way.

There should also be interesting sights to see on the walk, such as ancient walls, settlements or bridges. If you find a published route, there will be historical facts to read and sights to look out for.

TIPS AND CONSIDERATIONS

- Try to make the walk interesting and educational by doing some research beforehand; you'll then be able to have well-informed conversations about the history while you're walking.
- Take on small sections of an ancient road as part of a larger walk, or plan a longer walk that follows an ancient route as closely as possible.
- If walking a small section, use a map of an appropriate scale; rather than walk back along the road, make it a circular route.
- For a true test of endurance, attempt to follow a long section such as the well known Fosse Way from London to York.

AMY SAYS...

Sing a song while you're walking (using the tune of
One Man went to Mow, Went to Mow a Meadow).

One Roman went along, along a Roman road.
One Roman and his chariot went along the road.
Two Romans went along, along a Roman road.
Two men, one roman and his chariot went
along a Roman road.

See how many words you can make from the words
'Roman road' or any other Roman-related words.

DID YOU KNOW?

The Romans actually
named London but at
that time it was
called 'Londinium'.

Romans built straight
roads because it was the
fastest way to get their
troops from one place
to another.

BY THE SEA

Exploring the coastline, wherever you live, is one of the great childhood adventures that everyone remembers from their youth. Discover rock pools, peninsulas and tidal islands on foot by day, then sleep on the beach or on an island at night, after hours in the fresh air.

From crabbing to snorkelling, coasteering to cooking on a beach, there is simply no excuse for being bored while you are by the sea.

ADORE A PUFFIN

Find a coastline where you know that puffins nest, then try to spot one of these beautiful native birds in their natural habitat.

Spotting a rare animal or an endangered species in the wild is a rewarding and exciting experience; rewarding because you are likely to have gone to some lengths to catch a glimpse, and exciting because of the anticipation of your sighting.

Take your family out for the day on a challenge to see a specific rare animal and share the magic of the sighting together.

PUFFIN SPOTTING

Many people cite puffins as one of their favourite birds. Puffins are also one of the most easily identifiable seabirds in the UK. Despite this, not many people can say that they have actually seen them in the wild, with their own eyes.

The reason for this is that puffins are now becoming quite rare and their populations are in decline; partly due to the impact of extreme weather conditions. During the strong winds of Spring 2013, tens of thousands of puffins were washed up on the beaches along the northern coast of Northumberland and Yorkshire due to strong offshore winds, which prevented them from swimming or flying back to the cliffs to perch.

Consequently, they are now an Amber List species, according to the RSPB (Royal Society for the Protection of Birds). Check out their information page to learn all about puffins, where they live and when to see them.

TIPS AND CONSIDERATIONS

- Spend some time researching the animal or species you want to try and spot. Take into account the time of year, any breeding or hibernating patterns, nesting or weaning periods to ensure you maximize your chances of a sighting.
- Be respectful of the animal and its habitat. Encourage children to be aware of conservation. It's not a case of a sighting at all costs. Indeed, a sighting should be considered as an honour and only if it's in the best interests of an animal.

AMY SAYS...

WHO CAN STAY QUIET FOR THE LONGEST?

This is a game loved by many grown-ups because it is so peaceful and quiet. But in this instance, the aim of the game is crucial for spotting puffins. It's simple. Stay as silent and as still as you can for as long as you can to win the game, while hopefully spotting a Puffin. Also, MAKE SURE THE GROWN-UPS JOIN IN!

HAND SIGNALS

This game ties in perfectly with the one above. Create signals so that you can communicate with each other without talking. Make the signals simple so that they can be easily understood by other family members (e.g. parents!) and don't create too many, to avoid confusion.

ELLA'S JOKE

Which bird is always out of breath?

—

A puffin!

DID YOU KNOW?

As well as fish, Puffins eat something called Zooplankton.

CLEAN A BEACH

Visit a beach with the intention of making it cleaner than when you arrived.

Oceans and beaches exert a strong draw because of their wildness, their fresh sea air and other reasons too numerous to mention. For families wishing to spend a day at the beach, it is often the cleanliness of the beach and the sand that are key considerations in influencing how they all perceive, enjoy and value a beach environment.

Even though we all prefer to spend time on clean, litter-free beaches, such places are actually rare or impossible to find. This is because, despite how clean a beach looks, there is always a fair chance that there will be litter lurking around the high-tide line. Litter taints the look of the beach and poses a danger to people and wildlife.

The saddest fact is that rubbish on the high-tide line represents just a small proportion of the volume of litter that is floating around in our seas; the litter we see on beaches is just the tip of the iceberg.

BEACH CLEAN

Everyone but everyone, regardless of age or status, can do something about beach litter. In fact, the power of an ongoing, little-by-little collective effort is more likely to make a difference than a one-off organized activity. All it takes is for beach visitors to do just two things:

1 Take home any litter they generate during a visit to a beach (picnic, wrappers, drinks containers etc.).
2 Spend five or ten minutes at the high-tide line filling a dustbin bag of litter and then disposing of it responsibly.

If you do this every time you go to the beach, others will follow your example and over time, a change in behaviour could ultimately bring about a larger-scale moral 'sea-change'.

TIPS AND CONSIDERATIONS

- Wear shoes and gloves when walking around littered areas.
- If you have one, use a litter-picker.
- Empty children's buckets are useful receptacles for rubbish.

AMY SAYS...

BUILD A BARRIER GAME Choose a place quite far up the beach when the tide is coming in and start building a sand wall. Pat sand into a thick, long, sturdy barrier and stand behind it. When the tide eventually comes in, see if the wall stays up or if it crumbles down, getting you wet! Remember, never underestimate the tide's strength.

BUILD A SAND CAR Think you're good at building things out of sand? Well this challenge will really push your limits. Make a car out of compacted sand for a human to sit in.

DID YOU KNOW?

The longest beach in the world is the Praia do Cassino Beach in Brazil.

ELLA'S JOKE

What is a shark's favourite game?
—
Swallow the leader!

What do you find on a small beach?
—
Micro-waves!

COASTAL WALK

Walk along a portion of a coastal path until you reach a secluded beach. When you get there, go skinny dipping, if you dare!

One of the main advantages of living on an island like the UK is that you are never more than a few hours away from the coast.

With the coast so easily accessible to everyone, there really is no excuse not to take a trip to the sea. Here you can experience the fresh air, take in the exciting and often dramatic views, and feel the cool (often cold) but invigorating sea water against the skin.

Not all children like walking, but take them out along a coastal path with the promise of dropping down to a secluded beach along the way; or offer them sight of a working lighthouse perched precariously on a seat of rocks, and not many youngsters will be able to turn down your invitation. The chances of them coming across an ice-cream van are of course very high; and this always seems to be a motivator for children.

TIPS AND CONSIDERATIONS

- Walk on an established, maintained cliff path, rather than taking your own route along cliff tops.
- Children will naturally gravitate towards the edges of cliffs – and probably even ask to climb and scramble along them. Don't ever let them, as the chances of a fall or a cliff collapse are real.
- Check the tide times before you walk, particularly if you want to make the walk a circular one i.e. along the cliff tops and back along the beach (or vice versa).
- The weather at the coast can be a little bit unpredictable so make sure you go prepared for all weathers.
- It's a good idea to tell someone where you are going and when you plan to be back home – essential if you are planning to negotiate a route back along a beach, just in case the worst happens. You could get caught by the tide and cut off.
- Never let children throw rocks off a cliff top – there may be people or animals on the beach below.

AMY SAYS...

Don't have your swimming costume with you? No problem, go skinny dipping (swimming without any clothes on). No one will really mind, you're only a kid!

LOOK FOR FOSSILS They're common in cliffs made of mud or even in rocks. Watch out when you're under a cliff though – if it looks dangerous don't risk it, just go to another rock.

DID YOU KNOW?

Canada is the country with the longest coastline.

ELLA'S JOKE

How does the ocean
say goodbye?
—
It waves!

COASTEERING

Jump into water from the rocks then swim in between rocky islands and sea caves.

Coasteering is an increasingly popular adventure sport that combines scrambling, climbing and swimming along a rocky coastline. It may combine with optional, adrenaline-filled jumps from varying heights, depending on how brave you are! Suitable for almost all ages (seven or eight years and up) and abilities, this fun activity is a super way to see some of your own coastline from a different perspective.

While locals often explore their own coastlines, there are now quite a few adventure sports companies that offer guided sessions all over the country. It is advisable to go on a guided tour if you are not familiar with the tides, currents or weather conditions of a particular area. A tour will also highlight the safest and best locations at which to attempt the sport, and maybe pinpoint a whacky jump spot or a high-up launchpad.

When you're ready, put on a wetsuit, buoyancy aid and a helmet (all of which can be hired) plus a pair of old trainers that can be tied tightly, then clamber down the rocks to the coastline. Traverse up and down, rocks, admiring the wonders in rock pools and the views further afield. It is important to be aware of the tide; watch out for changes in the water level while scrabbling out of the water, as well as varying water depth when jumping into the sea. Don't forget rocks and barnacles can scrape the skin and cause damage to wetsuits, so an old pair of shorts worn over the wetsuit is an advisable addition to your wardrobe.

TIPS AND CONSIDERATIONS

- Always supervise young children on the rocks and in the water.
- Only jump into deep water; be aware that the sea level can change as the waves come in and out.
- When jumping, keep your arms tucked in, or crossed over your chest.
- Find easy routes out of the water.
- Stay with a buddy; help each other out of the water.
- Place any essentials (first aid kit, keys etc.) in a dry bag.

AMY SAYS...

When jumping into the sea, see
how silly you can look. Here are
some fun and crazy jumps to try:

- The superman
- The bomb-tuck jump
- 180°
- 360°
- The front or back flip — only do
  this if you are in a safe place and
  feeling confident.

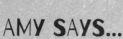

DID YOU KNOW?

Sea sponges are a form of
symbiotic algae.

COOK ON A BEACH

Living on an island means that there are plenty of beaches to choose from – sandy or rocky, large or small. The meal you cook can be part of a day or an evening on the beach, along with other activities.

The location of the beach will determine what you need to carry with you. Do you need to take fuel, such as kindling and wood, or can you collect it there? If you do collect wood before you go, then do so over a period of time, collecting twigs and sticks whenever you're out walking in woodlands. If you don't, then you'll need to spend some time collecting firewood once on the beach.

When you've found your secluded spot away from others, build a pit – a shallow hole in which the fire will be lit. Begin by lighting a small pyramid of kindling; you can do this the easy way with matches or lighter, or alternatively try using a fire lighter (steel and flint). To help get it started, add material that will catch light quickly, such as cotton wool. Adding petroleum jelly such as Vaseline, will also make the fire catch. Make sure that petroleum jelly is not on any fingers or lips, as they could catch light and cause severe injuries. Remember that fires are dangerous and must be respected. Children and adults should always be aware of keeping a safe distance and behave safely.

A fire is one option for cooking on a beach; you could always choose an easier option, such as a barbeque or a camping stove if you prefer. It is the location that is important and a beach is a wonderful place for a family meal out.

TIPS AND CONSIDERATIONS

- A fire needs heat, oxygen and fuel – create the right combination and you'll have a successful fire.
- Keep children a safe distance from the fire and be aware of any sparks.
- Don't leave the beach littered with rubbish or the remnants of a fire.
- Take some litter pickers and clean up the beach while you're there.

AMY SAYS...

Chocolate bananas are a great snack or dessert to cook on a campfire:

Push chocolate buttons into the skin of a banana (and eat a few while you're at it). Then wrap the banana in sheets of tinfoil. Place the food parcel on the fire to cook. The chocolate will melt and the banana will soften. Be careful when taking out the parcel — it will be hot, so use tongs (not tongues) or a fork. The foil will be hot, so remove this carefully too. Cut open the banana skin, then scoop out the hot chocolatey banana flesh with a spoon — yummy!

Instead of chocolate buttons, you could use a chocolate orange for a different flavour.

ELLA'S JOKE

What food is the best food to take to a beach?

—

Sandwiches!

DID YOU KNOW?

A burn from boiling water is worse than a dry burn received from a fire.

CRABBING

Dangle a line into the water and see if you can catch any crabs.

Crabbing is cheap and easy, yet so much fun. If carried out responsibly and sensibly it doesn't cause harm, unlike fishing and other 'catching' activities. In fact, the crabs should come out as the winners; the least they get is a little nibble on some tasty bait.

If you're on holiday and fancy going crabbing, ask the locals where to go; they'll know the best and safest places to go to with children, as well as the types of crabs you may catch. When crabbing off piers or slipways you are most likely to catch small green crabs; these are not edible and must be returned to sea before you go home.

TIPS AND CONSIDERATIONS

- Go crabbing as the tide starts to come in – the water is shallow and the crabs will start re-emerging from the sand.
- Make sure your bait bag or net sinks to the bottom. Crabs dwell on the sea floor and walk along the seabed looking for food.
- If your bait bag or net isn't sinking quickly enough, buy a cheap fishing weight and tie it to the bottom (or just put some small pebbles in it instead).
- Put the line over your finger and 'feel' for crabs nibbling at your bait.
- When you pull the net out to check, do so very slowly and carefully. Most crabs cling to the underside of the bag or net and will drop off if you pull too quickly.

WHAT YOU NEED

You actually need very little in the way of equipment; you certainly don't need anything expensive or specialized:

- A line (of some sort) with a small weight on it.
- Some bait – scraps of bacon or other meats are ideal – the smellier the better, as this will attract the crabs (they're not fussy eaters).
- Something to hold the bait in – the kind of net bags that hold washing powder tablets are ideal.
- A bucket or container to store the crabs in until you release them.

DID YOU KNOW?

There are 500 known species of hermit crabs.

NB For the health and well-being of the crabs, don't place too many of them in the same bucket. If any of them become aggressive to one another other, tip them all back into the sea straight away. It's a good idea to release the crabs after a short while anyway, so they don't get too stressed. You may catch them again later on!

ELLA'S JOKE

Who do young crabs want to see during the holidays?
—
Santa Claws!

AMY SAYS...

HAVE A CRAB RACE When you release the crabs into the water try to guess which one will win the race to the water's edge.

HOLD A CRAB This activity is quite simple but needs good technique to avoid getting nipped. Hold the crab from behind and put your thumb on top and your finger underneath. Using this technique, you hopefully won't get nipped.

EXPLORE A CAVE

Enter a cave and discover hidden treasures and unusual wildlife.

In a cave there are plenty of scrambling, climbing and camping opportunities for a family. It's also a good place for an exciting and adventurous walk. Even travelling to the cave adds an element of adventure and challenge. You usually have to trek across the countryside to discover its natural beauty and uncover its wildlife.

All caves are exciting, even those that may appear ordinary from the outside. Walk into a cave and you walk into an environment that feels very different to what we are used to. The temperature drops, sound becomes echoey and mysterious, and it is, of course, dark and eerie. Even an adult's imagination will run riot and begin to picture all kinds of beasts lurking and ready to pounce.

As well as their superb looks, caves give us an insight into our planet's geological past. It may be that a dry land cave was, millions of years ago, a coral reef streaming with oceanic life. A local cave may once have been underwater and even sat on the Equator, but as the tectonic plates of the Earth have moved and skewed, it may now sit far above sea level. There will always be a 'story' behind a cave, so ensure young adventurers are made aware of it, so that as they explore and investigate these natural playgrounds, they understand the process of their creation.

TIPS AND CONSIDERATIONS

- Caves are damp places and sometimes wet and muddy, so therefore slippery.
- Head torches are a good idea – for helping young ones to see, and be seen!
- Look out for cave life such as spiders and bats... and maybe even bears (OK, perhaps not).
- Sleeping in a cave will add an extra thrill and excitement to a visit. Take plenty of warm clothing though, as caves are often a lot cooler than the outdoor air temperature.
- Don't let children wander off too far on their own – caves can be disorientating and easy to get lost in.

AMY SAYS...

HAVE A SING SONG

'We're Going on a Bear Hunt' is a very well-known song that suits this situation perfectly. With a very easy tune, it's fun to sing the verse about the cave... if you dare! (Ask your parents if you don't know the song — they're bound to know it.)

DID YOU KNOW?

- The study of caves is called speleology.
- The most common type of cave is a solutional cave, created by acid in water that dissolves certain types of rock such as limestone.
- Throughout history, caves have been used as shelter, storage and burial grounds. Many paintings and treasures have been found in caves all over the world.

ELLA'S JOKE

What's grey, squeaky and hangs around in caves?
—
Stalagmice!

EXPLORE ROCK POOLS

Find some fresh, undisturbed rock pools and explore for signs of life.

The warmer summer weather brings with it more opportunities to take young children to the coast to enjoy some mini seaside adventures such as rock-pooling.

All you really need is a cheap fishing net and a bucket... oh, and a bit of luck.

Find out the tide times for the area in which you are going rockpooling. The best time to go is when the tide has turned and it's on its way out, leaving fresh, deep rock pools. If you are unsure of tide times, keep an idea of what the sea is doing and ensure you are able to retreat safely should the tide start to creep up around you – you don't want to be cut off from dry land.

TIPS AND CONSIDERATIONS

The surfaces that surround rock pools can be slippery due to the moisture left in the seaweed and on the stones. It is a good idea to wear suitable footwear to prevent slipping and to protect against getting grazed and cut feet.

A FEW TIPS FOR YOUNG ROCK POOL EXPLORERS

Keep as quiet as you can
- Move slowly and avoid casting shadows on the pools.
- Sit and watch as if you weren't really there.... that's when the inhabitants start to move about.
- Be careful when catching and handling sea life – you don't want to damage anything.
- Try to put things back where you found them as soon as you've had a look at them.

To start with, rock pools may look empty but don't give up. Be patient and keep still, then you'll soon start spotting stuff.

AMY SAYS...
WHAT YOU MIGHT FIND

- **CRABS**   These bury themselves in the sand and hide under rocks and weed.

- **FISH**   They dart around very quickly, often around the edges of the pool.

- **SEA ANEMONES**   Jelly-like in appearance, they stick to rocks and often have flowery, tentacled tops. Most are harmless but for some, this species can be toxic, so don't touch them!

- **LIMPETS**   Grey/white shells that stick to rocks when the tide is out.

- **HERMIT CRAB**   A shy crab that lives inside a shell and rarely comes out if disturbed.

Don't forget to replace any stones that you move and don't poke any of the sea life — you wouldn't like it if it were you!

DID YOU KNOW?

Rock pools are created by the sea coming in and filling up holes in the coastline.

ELLA'S JOKE

Which fish is the most famous?
—
The starfish!

RIDE A WAVE

Catch a wave or two on a bodyboard. Try and avoid being rinsed!

Bodyboarding is a great activity for all ages. At a beach the more energetic and adventurous visitor doesn't sit around sunbathing, but hits the water to try and catch a few waves.

The two things needed for bodyboarding are a board and a wetsuit. Bodyboards can be bought easily in many seaside tourist shops or sports shops.

Before starting to bodyboard there is a natural progression of skills to conquer. First of all, practice jumping over the waves, gradually getting deeper and deeper. Then practice swimming with the wave before trying to use a bodyboard. Who knows, you might end up progressing to standing up on a surfboard!

When heading out into the waves, hold the board to the side of your body; this avoids getting a face full of board when the waves arrive. When you're ready to launch off, try to be travelling at the same speed as the wave as it approaches you. The board needs to be slightly in front of the breaking wave. Kick your legs to keep up with the force of the water and then remember to cling on as you ride the wave!

TIPS AND CONSIDERATIONS

- Stick to the area between the yellow and red flags, where there is lifeguard patrol.
- Look out for other bodyboarders and swimmers. They'll be fighting for the same waves but you don't want to clash in the water.
- Avoid putting your weight too far forward or else you'll be put through the rinse cycle!
- Don't just travel in a straight line but keep looking for the best part of the wave to ride on; tilting the board will allow you to steer and change the direction that you are travelling in.

AMY SAYS...

Have a 'longest wave' competition. Pick a wave that everyone will ride together. See who can keep going for the furthest distance.

When walking to and from the water, remember to carry your board in as cool a manner as you can. Practice saying, 'dude' in as many sentences as you can — it's a word you can add to any sentence for dude-tastic effect!

ELLA'S JOKE

How do surfers say 'hi' to each other?

—

They wave!

SURF TALK

TUBE The tunnel created as the wave curls over.

SURF The waves.

SURF'S UP The conditions are good for surfing.

RAD Amazing!

WIPEOUT When everything goes wrong!

SEAL WATCHING

Spend some time observing and appreciating seals in their natural habitat.

Seals are one of the best-loved marine mammals and are often a firm favourite with children. Their inquisitive nature and adorable eyes charm anyone lucky enough to have an encounter with them, whether observing them basking on a rock in the sunshine or popping their heads up out of the water to survey visitors on the beach.

There are over 30 different species of seals around the world but two species can commonly be found on the coastline around Britain – the grey and common seals. When spotting seals, it can be difficult to tell the difference between the two; the main difference can be seen on the head: common seals have smaller heads and shorter muzzles, with nostrils that form a V-shape; whereas grey seals have longer muzzles and parallel nostrils.

Seal sanctuaries are great places to visit for seeing seals up close and to learn about them, but there's nothing quite like watching wild seals in their natural habitat. And you don't have to go on expensive boat trips or travel to exotic places to see wild seals.

While you might spot seals frollicking in the sea or lounging lazily on a beach by chance, there are certain locations, at specific times of the year, where you are guaranteed a sighting. In fact, during the late autumn many seaside locations have an abundance of grey seal colonies with their newly born pups. Grey seal pups are born on land and have attractive white coats. If visiting one of these locations, there are often information boards that provide a great source of photographs, updates on the seal colony and interesting information. As well as seeing pups close-up, there is also plenty of other action to witness; male bulls and female cows bickering and squabbling over territory, some more aggressive acts and posturing, as well as chasing, rolling and cow and pup bonding.

For children with an interest in wildlife, watching seals at a seaside location is the perfect outdoor natural exhibit.

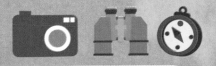

TIPS AND CONSIDERATIONS

- Allow plenty of time to observe seals.
- Respect the seals' environment and don't make loud noises or fast movements.

AMY SAYS...
TAKE ONE PICTURE
See who can capture the best picture of a seal. Try to capture good moments, because a photo of a seal sitting down on its own is a pretty boring photo. Seal pups are always winners because they are so cute, so try and catch the adorable things that they are doing. Choose someone who didn't enter the competition to judge the best one.

ELLA'S JOKE
Why do seals swim in salt water?
—
Because pepper water makes them sneeze!

DID YOU KNOW?
Some seals hold their breath for nearly two hours underwater!

SLEEP ON A BEACH

Spend a night under the stars in a bivvi bag on a beach.

Rather than returning home at the end of a day on the beach, why not light a fire, have a meal and then set up for the night for a real family adventure.

Finding a suitable beach isn't as easy, or as romantic, as it sounds. Even though there are numerous beaches surrounding the country, selecting an appropriate one needs careful consideration. It is important to know the times of the high tide and to have easy access to an escape route if space is limited. Weather conditions can also affect choices, so it is worth checking the weather forecast before planning to camp out on a beach. Also, be sure to check that the beach isn't infested by sand fleas – these can be pretty nasty! They

may not be visible during the day, but they tend to come out at night – just as you're settling down to sleep!

Once bedding arrangements are set up (tents, bivvi bags, hammocks etc.), you are lulled to sleep by the sounds of crashing waves and then woken in the morning by an alarm of seabirds. Additional treats may include seal sightings or stargazing in the middle of the night.

The next morning, after breakfast outdoors, go for a dip in the sea if conditions are right and you are daring enough.

TIPS AND CONSIDERATIONS

- Know the tidal times.
- Have a clear route in and out of the beach.
- Research weather conditions – if you don't manage it the first time you can always try again another time.
- Take some litter pickers and do your bit – pick up any litter (often on the high tide line) to take away with you.

AMY SAYS...

STONE DRAWINGS This is art stepped up a gear. Drawing on paper with a pencil is easy compared to this creative challenge. Find a largish stone (slate is best) and find a smaller, thin slither of slate. Then find something you want to draw. Being on a beach is quite an advantage as the cliffs and the rocky coast usually offer stunning views. Once you are satisfied with your choice of scenery, start scratching the picture onto the stone. Don't worry if your first attempt isn't very good; it takes time to become an amazing artist.

The other option, apart from drawing, is to find a big stone and some little shells. Collect as many little shells as you want and when you get home, stick them on to the stone.

DID YOU KNOW?

A group of sand fleas can whine at such a high pitch that humans can hear them!

ELLA'S JOKE

What do you call a plated dinosaur when he is asleep?

—

Stegosnorus!

SLEEP ON AN UNINHABITED ISLAND

Canoe or sail to an island and spend the night there.

A mini expedition to an island involves careful planning and consideration. Firstly, how are you going to get to the island? Are you going to take, borrow or hire your means of transport? It could be canoes or a sailing boat, but ideally it should be something that is able to transport the family as well as all your provisions.

The journey is as much a part of the adventure as anything. Consider the location and the distance you need to travel; this may be affected by weather, tides and, of course, physical abilities. Working as a team to paddle or sail to the destination is all part of it! The very nature of travelling to an uninhabited island means that there will be few people, and hopefully a wonderful environment to discover together.

When packing, you will need to consider clothing for different weather conditions, a first aid kit, sleeping equipment, food and cooking equipment. This will all have to fit into your canoe or boat, so plan carefully and take only what you really need.

Islands obviously vary in size, so picking a spot to set up camp will be one of the first decisions, after an exciting exploration!

Decide where to set up the sleeping area, where to cook and finally the entertainment – what is there to do on the island?

TIPS AND CONSIDERATIONS

- Only pack what you need; the kitchen sink won't be much use! Be prepared for different weather conditions and temperature changes and take layers of clothing. Pyjamas are a luxury that you can do without.
- Take dry bags to avoid getting any kit wet. Think about where to pack equipment so that it won't get splashed or can be easily accessible if needed.
- Pull the boat up and out of the water, in case there is a change in water level.
- Consider the direction and strength of the wind – build a fire downwind of the camp.
- Respect the environment in which you are in; remember the well-known saying, 'Take only photographs and leave only footprints'.

DID YOU KNOW?

In Japan, Hashima Island aka Battleship Island, (hence its shape), used to have over 5000 residents until it was abandoned. It is now uninhabited but open to tourists, as all the old buildings still stand there.

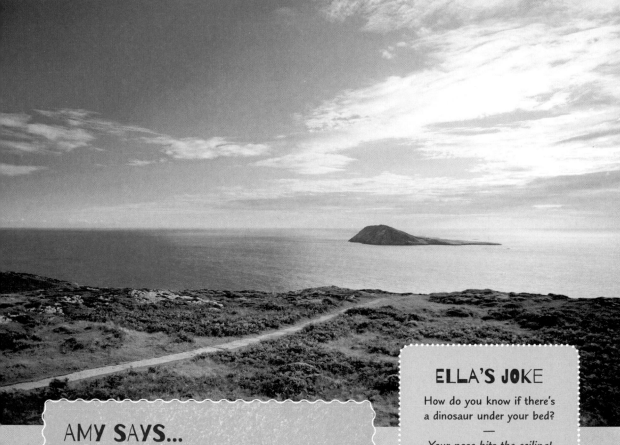

ELLA'S JOKE

How do you know if there's a dinosaur under your bed?

—

Your nose hits the ceiling!

AMY SAYS...

Spend time fully exploring the island. Go around it lots of times trying out different routes. You could turn this into a game and play Follow the Leader!

OTHER THINGS TO DO

- Find the best tree to climb.
- Spy on any passing boats. Make a messaging language to communicate with, that only you know.
- Draw a map of the island and make up names for any beaches or bays on it.
- Hide treasure on the island and challenge each other to find it (using the map!).

SNORKELLING

Put on a snorkel and a mask and explore sea waters.

A cheap and cheerful way to explore life under the water is by snorkelling; it requires neither the equipment nor the training demanded of scuba diving. In fact, you can often get the best view of the sea nearest the surface, where the sun lights up the plants and the most colourful fish dwell. In warmer climates, the most dramatically coloured corals can be found in the shallower waters.

The main equipment needed for snorkelling is a mask and a snorkel. These can often be bought in seaside tourist shops and do not cost a fortune. Flippers (fins) are also a good idea because they take away some of the effort needed to swim. In colder waters, and even in hotter climates, it is always a good idea to wear a wetsuit; it keeps you warmer, repels the sun and reassures the less confident snorkeller against jellyfish stings.

Snorkelling can be enjoyed by people of all ages and abilities, in warm and cold waters. You can learn a few techniques in a swimming pool and leisure centres sometimes offer taster courses that cover a few basic techniques. Weak or non-swimmers can join in too if they wear a buoyancy aid. Snorkelling has many similarities to scuba diving; when swimming you adopt a similar posture: you don't use your arms (they're crossed) and you kick slowly with the legs. When more confident, try diving down under the water – hold your breath. When you come up, breath out and blow water out of the snorkel.

DID YOU KNOW?

There are about 11 million snorkellers in the United States and about 20 million snorkellers around the world!

TIPS AND CONSIDERATIONS

- Go snorkelling from a beach, off rocks or further out, from a kayak.
- Snorkel with a buddy.
- Supervise kids when snorkelling.
- Seek local knowledge – avoid strong currents and find out tidal times.
- Don't touch, prod or poke anything under the water, and never take anything away with you.

ELLA'S JOKE

Why do seagulls fly over the sea?
—
Because if they flew over the bay they would be called bagels!

TOP TIP Spit into your mask and rub it around. Swill it out and put it on. It sounds a bit disgusting, but it should stop your mask steaming up!

AMY SAYS...

Divers keep a log of every dive they do. In it they record where they dived, at what time and what they saw. You could do the same with snorkelling; create your own snorkelling log. You could buy a disposable waterproof camera and take photographs of the fish and plants that you see and add them to your log.

Divers have to communicate with hand signals, for obvious reasons! Try to learn some of the basic hand signals and go to www.divers.net for illustrations.

- OK Are you ok?/Yes I'm ok (see right).

- OK WITH BOTH HANDS Yes I'm excellent.

- THUMBS UP I want to go up.

- THUMBS DOWN I want to go down.

- HAND ON HEAD Shark.

WALK A PENINSULA

Walk the full length of a peninsula and appreciate the sights, smells and sounds.

A peninsula is simply an area of land bordered by water on three sides while remaining connected to the mainland. There are many peninsulas to walk around in the UK and the wider world, so you are never too far away from one. Put 'walk around a peninsula' into your family adventure diary one weekend!

The fact that most kids love beaches makes this a winner of an activity; they will just keep walking and walking, playing and exploring on the beach, not realizing they are doing a peninsula walk at all!

On a more serious note, a walk on a beach is, literally, never the same on any two occasions. The landscape, or sandscape, is in constant flux from the wind, water and human impacts. There's always something interesting to see...

be it the stones and pebbles and their array of shapes and colours, or the views out to sea of migrating birds, busy fishing boats or slow-moving transporter ships that are keeping the nation going with the supplies they carry.

Sadly, peninsulas are often traps for all things that float around in the ocean. Consequently it may be litter that is one of the strongest memories you take away with you. One of humankind's most useful and yet suffocating of creations – plastic – blights the world's coastlines.

Don't let this deter you though, walk a peninsula with your kids and enjoy the views, the smells and the thoughtful conversations that such an environment will inspire.

TIPS AND CONSIDERATIONS

- Take binoculars with you, as peninsulas offer great views of ocean sea and birdlife.
- If there is a lot of litter and rubbish about, make sure youngsters are wearing something on their feet.
- Discourage children from picking up unknown objects.
- Look for shells and fossils in the high tide line.

AMY SAYS...

EAT A TANKER Take along a camera and stage a photo. If you see a tanker or submarine, stand sideways, make it look like you are holding it and open you mouth. When the tanker crawls slowly towards your open mouth, it will look like you're eating it, so take the picture.

CONTAINER SHIP CLUEDO Look for clues on the passing container ships and try and work out (or predict or imagine) which country and city they are from, what they are carrying and how long it might take them to get to their destination.

ELLA'S JOKE

What do you get if a dinosaur walks across a strawberry patch?

—

Strawberry jam!

DID YOU KNOW?

As of 2014, there are nearly 80 million people living on the Arabian Peninsula.

WALK TO A TIDAL ISLAND

Find out the times of the tides and walk to an island when the tide is low.

A tidal island is one that can only be reached when the tide is out; at other times it is cut off from the mainland. Some tidal islands are linked to the mainland via a manmade causeway, allowing access for bikes and vehicles – as well as cyclists and pedestrians.

Such causeways offer an opportunity for a visit to the island, and an exciting game of cat and mouse with the sea when returning to the mainland, before the tide cuts off the causeway.

Lindisfarne Island, or the Holy Island, is one of the best known tidal islands in the UK and is a super location for a family trip and a race against the tide.

OTHER WELL-KNOWN TIDAL ISLANDS

Small islets on the Menai Straits linked to the Isle of Anglesey, Wales. Mont St Michel, France.

AMY SAYS...

CAR WATCH Watch and egg on drivers who leave a dash back to the mainland as late as possible. Make sure you aren't the cause of their car breaking down when there is lots of water sluicing across the road.

BEACH WATCH Predict and guess the movements of the sea — it's fascinating to see how the tide eventually swallows up the beach in a surprisingly short time.

Take a crabbing net and fish for crabs that will emerge from the sand as the tide turns.

TIPS AND CONSIDERATIONS

- Make sure you check the tide charts so that you attempt to cross during the 'safe-crossing window'.
- Local bus services often run between the mainland and tidal islands. Use these services to ensure you can get to and from the mainland.
- Never take risks while trying to beat the tide, especially if you have children with you.
- If you are ever in danger of being cut off by the incoming tide, phone for help as soon as you can, and try as a last resort to look for an emergency tower along the causeway.

DID YOU KNOW?

The Holy island in Northumberland attracts over 650,000 visitors per year from around the world despite having only 160 residents!

ELLA'S JOKE

Why didn't the shrimp
have any friends?

—

Because he was a bit shellfish!

EXTREME WEATHER

When the weather turns freezing how about wrapping up warm and going out exploring in the snow? Perhaps you can learn to cook with snow or play in snow drifts. Look at your own locality in a new light by setting out on a sledge safari or starting a snow expedition. Or maybe you'd like to indulge in a spot of sub-zero camping, taking on the elements?

COOK WITH SNOW

Cook with snow when out in the winter weather.

Being able to sustain yourself when out and about on an adventure is a key element of survival – particularly when the weather conditions are grim, or when you need to re-fuel mid-adventure. When adventurers go on expeditions they have to take large quantities of packaged food and water with them in order to survive. But if the conditions are icy or snowy, the need to take water isn't so great, because there is a ready supply close at hand. A warming cup of something is a rewarding treat for the intrepid explorer.

When you are next out on a snowy family adventure, plan a stop-off for a simple meal or a snack. If you head out for a winter walk or a sledge safari during snowy conditions, pack a small stove, a pan and some packets of freeze-dried food, such as packets of powdered soup. When you decide to stop, fill the pan with snow and heat it up. Once boiling, the water can be added to any soup powder and drunk out of mugs. Don't forget to take along some bread for dipping too. You could also make a more substantial meal: add pasta to the melted water and bring to the boil. Add a simple tomato sauce and eat out of your mugs or bowls.

In other parts of the world, where snow is a common occurrence, families make treats with snow, such as ice cream. By mixing cream or milk, sugar and vanilla with fresh snow, you can create your own homemade ice cream as a satisfying treat.

TIPS AND CONSIDERATIONS

- Use clean snow; avoid yellow snow!
- Don't eat cold snow – it will lower your body temperature.
- Encourage the kids to be in charge of the cooking.

DID YOU KNOW?

Drinking and eating frozen snow can actually make you more dehydrated than you were before!

ELLA'S JOKE

How do snowmen travel around?
—
By icicle!

AMY SAYS...

Following the cooking theme, test your artistic abilities by creating crockery that could be used in the kitchen.

Use compact snow to mould into different shapes like cups and bowls. Then, collect different things like stones or wood chippings and see how strong your models are. Are there different shapes of snow pottery that are stronger?

PLAY IN SNOWDRIFTS

Dive and tumble in snowdrifts, and make snow holes and shelters.

When the snow is too wet, too cold and frozen, or too dry to build a snowman in or to go sledging, then you will have to go looking for snowdrifts to play in. A spell of heavy snow, accompanied by viciously cold and very strong winds will mean only one thing: snowdrifts!

Deep and dramatic snowdrifts are great fun to play in. Walking through them is harder than it might sound, jumping into them never gets boring, and digging into them can result in a sheltered snow hole.

When everyone else is inside, cosy in front of the television, get wrapped up and head out into your local area looking for drifts that might have accumulated at the leeward (down wind) side of walls, or filled and covered ditches between fields.

Have fun exploring the drifts but do make sure that everyone is aware of how to keep safe in deep snow and to keep an eye out for collapsing snow or ice.

TIPS AND CONSIDERATIONS

- Beware of the effects of wind chill, which is the perceived difference in air temperature due to the flow of cold air.
- Wind jammer or wind stopper clothing helps prevent wind chill from lowering the body temperature.
- Local knowledge will help ensure playing in snowdrifts is a safe activity; when children are jumping into snowdrifts, it is best to know what might lie beneath the surface.
- If youngsters try and dig a snow hole into a snowdrift, stay close at hand just in case it collapses: snow and ice are heavy, and being trapped under snow is dangerous.
- Take your dogs out with you; they are likely to have as much fun in the drifts as you do!

ELLA'S JOKE

What's the biggest problem
with snow boots?
—
They melt!

AMY SAYS...

JUMP INTO SNOWDRIFTS Some drifts are really
deep and are perfect for playing and jumping in. Compact some
snow into a podium and start a competition. Have separate
categories like 'Who can do the best jump?' or 'Who can land
the furthest in?' Avoid coloured snow — it's no fun if you land
in something yucky under the surface of the drift!

DIG A SNOW SHELTER, AKA A SNOW HOLE
Deep drifts are again needed in this challenge. Snow holes are
handy things to know how to make and you might need to make
one when out on an expedition so have fun practising. Dig quite
far into the side of the drift and make the hole wide enough for the
amount of people that need to fit in (it may need to be quite a lot
bigger if adults have to fit in your shelter). Try and make the sides
as strong as possible by compacting snow in.

DID YOU KNOW?

On long expeditions,
explorers use snow holes
to sleep in and to keep
warm. They sometimes
wake up to find that snow
has collapsed and blocked
the door, then they have
to dig to get to the exit.

SLEDGE SAFARI

Explore your local area for unspoilt sledging opportunities – away from the crowds.

With the downfall of heavy snow comes the opportunity to adventure out into your locality to get to know it a bit better. Normally you navigate around your local area using footpaths and roads, but when these are all snowed under, you can wander around more freely looking for gradients rather than grey matter underfoot.

Grab a sledge and go out looking for unusual and unsuspecting locations in which to take a sledge ride. The aim of this adventure is to sledge new slopes for the first time.

It's a bit like the way in which a skateboarder sees the urban landscape differently to other people. You and your children will notice gradients and undulations that you never knew existed: a sloping road, a cut-through between some houses, a piece of sloping rough ground that you never usually walk on. You'll be amazed at how differently you will see such a familiar place.

TIPS AND CONSIDERATIONS

- Make sure children always check the safety of a new slide before they try it. Looking at where the slope might take them and what the end speed will be.
- Make sure sledgers are kitted up with gloves, hats and padded clothing to protect them from any bumps and scrapes (as well as the cold).
- Avoid sledging on private land, including other people's gardens.
- Look for unsledged routes. If there is somebody already there, move on to a new location.

DID YOU KNOW?

In ancient Egypt, sledges were used to haul blocks of stone!

AMY SAYS...

Think of some really 'radical' names for your newly discovered runs such as 'Deadly Drop' for a fairly steep slope.

If your sledge is broken, or the shops have sold out, make your own sledge out of things you can find at home using cardboard, thick plastic sheet and some duct tape. It's also important to have something to use as a brake.

See how many people you can cram onto one sledge then ride a slope together.

ELLA'S JOKE

Why did the snowman call his dog Frost?

—

Because Frostbites!

SNOW EXPEDITION

Transport your kit on a sledge and head off for a trek in the snow.

Don't waste the precious time in your life clearing your drive of snow – instead get wrapped up and go on a mini expedition. It's much more fun!

OK so this is no trip to the North Pole. You are venturing into your local area after a heavy downfall of snow – but you'll be surprised at how exciting and exhilarating this simple adventure idea is for everyone.

Take a sledge of any kind and use a couple of roof-rack straps, or a piece of rope, to create a simple harness that will allow someone to pull the sledge behind them. The kids, or young polar explorers as we shall now call them, should really start feeling the part now. Tie a backpack containing rations, water and other essentials onto the sledge, and find some walking poles (all polar explorers have walking poles) – and you are ready to go.

Preparing in this way, along with the right cold and snowy weather conditions, makes a walk into the local fields feel like a full-on mini expedition.

TIPS AND CONSIDERATIONS

- Plan an expedition into an area in walking distance; forcing you to walk door to door.
- Head out into fields and open space away from roads and people – it will feel more dramatic and exciting for your young explorers.
- Avoid parental instincts to help the young explorers get their kit over obstacles like ditches and field boundaries – let them struggle (in the nicest possible way).

AMY SAYS...

This adventure is actually great fun for us kids. Towing a sledge loaded with supplies makes you feel like a real explorer; it makes you feel alive. Lugging sleds through thick snow gives you a taste of real expeditions such as 'Scott's expedition to the Arctic' and the cold conditions make it feel like you're trying to survive and have all your belongings on a sledge you're towing. This adventure through a kid's eyes may be very different to an adult's.

FORBIDDEN OBJECT GAME Try not to think about a certain object of your choice and shout it out for the rest of the players to hear. This is actually harder than it seems, because by trying too hard, you remember what you were trying to avoid thinking of. Try too little and you'll think of the 'forbidden' object anyway! Every time you think of it, say 'ooh'.

ELLA'S JOKE

What do you call young dogs who play in the snow?
—
Slush puppies!

DID YOU KNOW?

Snow reflects a lot of ultraviolet radiation and can cause snow blindness. Sunglasses and goggles help protect the eyes by absorbing some of the rays.

SNOW HIKE

After a heavy snowfall, hike to a local village and catch the bus home.

We, like most people I would imagine, rarely explore our immediate locality – especially when going for a decent walk of any length. We tend to drive somewhere and then walk. As this adventure shows though, you can achieve a sense of exploration and discovery by simply setting off from your doorstep and walking back again via a local village or place of interest.

This adventure can take place at any time of the year, but it is particularly enjoyable and interesting when carried out after a significant snowfall.

When everybody else is clearing their drive and brushing snow off their cars (yawn), leave your vehicle on the drive and head out on foot across the fields and footpaths in your local area. And if you do so on a snowy winter's day, you'll be sure to see animal tracks, spectacular snowscapes and stunning snow-dressed plants and trees, so do enjoy the experience of walking across large expanses of pure, virgin snow.

Take some birdseed and leave piles of food on footpath marker posts – the birds will benefit and your young walkers will become so much more aware of the route the path is taking. This is another benefit of walking in your local area; your children will see this familiar landscape from a different and fresh

perspective – great for the body and mind but also great for developing their sense of space, place and locality.

A snowy landscape makes this a magical adventure, but the sense of exploration and adventure will be felt at any time of the year.

TIPS AND CONSIDERATIONS

- Wearing plastic bags on top of your socks will ensure tootsies are warm even if your shoes or boots don't keep the wet out.
- Remember to take some loose change for the bus home.

AMY SAYS...

MAKE A SNOW ANGEL

A classic snow activity that never gets tiresome. Basically, lie down in the snow and push your arms from your side up in line with your shoulders and push your legs out and in together again. Repeat this process until you have formed an angel shape. To get up, pull your arms in and either have a hand-up to avoid pushing on the angel or push your arms outside the body line of the snow angel and push up.

PLAY 'PINE CONES' AND 'TWIGS'
When having a rest in the snow, make a noughts and crosses (tic-tac-toe) board and play 'pine cones and twigs' — an environmentally friendly version of the classic game.

DID YOU SNOW?

Never eat yellow snow — or even touch it if you can help it!

ELLA'S JOKE

Where do penguins go to dance?
—
The snow ball!

SUB-ZERO CAMPING

Sub-zero camping is something that's associated with intrepid explorers battling icy conditions in the Antarctic. Most people admit to being fair-weather campers and dust off their tents in late spring or early summer, but who says camping shouldn't be an all-year-round activity even in a country with unpredictable weather conditions? There is a saying: 'There is no bad weather, only bad clothing'. Well, you could apply this to camping in sub-zero temperatures – you have just got to be prepared. Nobody enjoys being cold, but don't let that put you off, because you won't be too chilly if you have the right clothing.

If you are going to brave camping outdoors in sub-zero temperatures, you need to wrap up warm. You don't need specialist camping equipment – a simple tent, a regular sleeping bag and a roll mat are more than adequate. In addition you will need layers of clothing for further warmth, including thick socks, thermals, fleeces and neck warmers.

For the first attempt, it might be a good idea to try it in the back garden or somewhere local. Even in the back garden, it will feel like something extreme and exciting. If you are camping on a site or indulging in wild camping, select a spot sheltered from the wind; any wind chill will add discomfort to the experience, so try to avoid it.

When you wake in the morning, after a refreshing night in the cold air, you will probably be able to see your breath. Unzip the tent and find out if the canvas is covered in a layer of frost or ice.

TIPS AND CONSIDERATIONS

- Wear layers of clothing rather than one big heavy coat or jumper.
- Don't forget the extremities – a hat, neck warmer, gloves and a good pair of socks add to the comfort.

DID YOU KNOW?

Ice is made up of tiny little crystals!

AMY SAYS...

ICE DECORATIONS When you wake up in the morning, look on the side of your tent and you may see ice crystals scattered around on the canvas from the night before. In the morning sun, they may glisten and look beautiful, almost like decorations on your tent.

MAKE YOUR OWN ICE DECORATIONS Place cookie cutters on plates, fill with natural materials such as berries, pebbles etc. plus a piece of string. Then add water. The water will freeze in the night and you should be able to remove your decoration and hang it on a tree.

ELLA'S JOKE

Why is it cold at Christmas?

—

Because it's in Decembrrrr!

TAKE ON THE ELEMENTS

When everyone else is indoors, get kitted up and take on the elements.

Poor weather can often put paid to a family outing. The threat of a heavy downpour or strong winds has the potential to scupper a planned adventure. However, try to see a horribly wet or cold day as an opportunity for a challenge, and go out there to take on the elements! A long or strenuous walk in lashing rain, whipping wind or horrendous hail will feel like a battle at the time, but it is a battle that will give you the reward of a well-earned sense of satisfaction.

Challenging conditions might include heavy rain, strong winds, cold conditions, heavy underfoot conditions, or any combination of the aforementioned.

Taking on the elements is straightforward; you have only three main considerations:

1 Keep dry
2 Keep warm
3 Keep safe

Keeping dry and warm requires you to wear appropriate clothing which keeps water and wind out, but body heat in. Keeping safe requires you to make sensible decisions with regards to conditions, the age of the youngsters in your care, and knowing when to call it a day and retire to the comfort of somewhere warm and dry.

TIPS AND CONSIDERATIONS

- Children and adults will soon feel cold and miserable if they become wet, so try to beg, borrow or buy suitable clothing for your adventure; Gortex outer clothing and boots make a big difference.
- Encourage a 'don't give in' attitude, but equally important, encourage youngsters to know that calling off a challenge for safety reasons is the bravest decision you can make.
- Family adventures are meant to be fun, but on this occasion it is important to try and develop some steel and determination; expect some moaning and whining during the adventure.

AMY SAYS...

Sing songs to keep you in good spirits and take your mind off the pain to make you believe you can do it. Examples include:

'We Will Rock You'
'I Get Knocked Down But I Get Up Again'

Make the wind hold you — face the wind and start to lean slightly against it. See how much weight you can put against it. Be aware of the fact that the wind might drop suddenly and you might fall over, so have someone nearby to catch you (don't make the person stand in front of you, as they will block the wind!).

DID YOU KNOW?

The highest amount of rain that ever fell in 24 hours was in Cilaos, Reunion, in the Indian Ocean in 1952, when 187cm (73 inches) fell.

ELLA'S JOKE

What do you call a grizzly bear caught in the rain?
—
A drizzly bear!

INDEX

FOR SALLY

Thank you to the following for helping us with this endeavour:

Our parents.

Simon Meek and First Burgh St Peter and Raveningham Sea Scouts
for the loan of their raft building equipment.

Robin, Kathryn, Peter, Jo and the kids for a memorable,
entertaining night, camping out on the top of a mountain.

Matt Heason for providing us with beautiful photographs to illustrate
some of the adventures that his family have also done.

Adrian Sington and DCD media for believing in us.

Tentsile for providing us with an exciting, alternative sleeping method.

Alpkit for getting us essential kit items such as bivvi bags.

RAB for decent sleeping bags that allow us to camp out in all weathers.

Alastair Humphreys for inspiring us with his microadventures.

Frances Lincoln Ltd
www.franceslincoln.com

100 Family Adventures
Copyright © Frances Lincoln 2015
Text copyright © Tim, Kerry, Amy and Ella Meek

First Frances Lincoln edition 2015

Tim, Kerry, Amy and Ella Meek have asserted their right
to be indentified as the authors of this work in accordance
with the Copyright, Designs and Patents Act 1988 (UK).

A catalogue record for this book is available from the British Library.

ISBN 978-0-7112-3661-5

Printed and bound in China

9 8 7 6 5 4 3 2 1

This book contains some potentially dangerous activities. Please note
that any reader or anyone in their charge taking part in any of the activities
described does so at their own risk. Neither the authors nor the publisher
can accept any legal responsibility for any harm, injury, damage, loss or
prosecution resulting from the use or misuse of the activities in the book.

It is illegal to carry out any of these activities on private land without
the owner's permission, and you should obey all laws relating
to the protection of land, property, plants and animals.